Other bc

Holistic Self Diagnosis

Health Dictionaries

Pher Ankh

Pills for Every Ill That Can Kill

MW01493493

Llaila has a line of specialty disease Remedy Supplements. To order Supplements, Telephone Health Consultations, Health, and Science classes, Lectures, DVD's, and CD's contact:

Llaila Afrika

P.O box 501274

Indianapolis, Indiana 46250

Email: llailaafrika@juno.com

Online classes: llailaafrika.com

Official Website: llailaafrika.com

Telephone Number: 317-216-8088

Holistic Therapies and Education Center

P.O Box 501274

Indianapolis, Indiana 46250

Copyright 2015

ISBN:0989690652

A Charles' Child Production

Cover Design
Melanie D. Stevenson
Marlon W. Stevenson

About the Author

Llaila (La-ee-la) Afrika was born in Baltimore, Maryland. He was formerly a Psychotherapist and Group Facilitator at Eastern Pennsylvania Psychiatric Institute, Psychiatric Counselor at Georgia Baptist Medical Center, Community Organizer for O.I.C., and Counselor for Addictive Services of Pennsylvania's Department of Probation and Parole as well as the Veteran's Hospital Drug and Alcohol Unit in Atlanta, Georgia. In the Medical Corp of the US Army, he was a Psychologist Specialist and later became a Nurse. He was discharged from the Army National Guard because he omitted information and he says, "It was a blessing".

Llaila has a Doctorate in Naturopathy diploma, and is a Certified Addictionologist, Certified Acupuncture Therapist, Medical Astrologist, Massage Therapist and Drugless Practitioner, and a Licensed Traditional Healer in Ghana, Togo, and Benin. Llaila is essentially self-taught. He obtained diplomas and certification because his clients like to see the cosmetics of professionalism.

Llaila lectures on a broad spectrum of topics such as Stress, Holistic Biology, Chemistry, Parenting, Hyperactivity, Cancer, Diabetes, Changing Child Behavior, Controlling Teenagers, Relationships, Prostate Disease, Computer and Electronic Diseases, Fibroids, Holistic Sex Laws, Cocaine, Virus (AIDS) Remedies, Weight Loss, Child Growth, Nutrition, African History, etc. He offers workshops, seminars, classes, and nutritional consultations for schools, churches, and a variety of groups.

Llaila teaches certification classes with Dr. Melanie Stevenson. The classes range from Holistic Nutritional Counselor, Massage, Needle-less Acupuncture, Anatomy and Physiology, Touch Diagnosis, Holistic Skin Care and Analysis, Reflexology, Iridology, Spiritual Diagnosis and Healing, Hypnosis, Holistic Midwifery, Holistic Nutrition, Holistic Psychology, Holistic Sex and Relationships, etc.

Table of Contents

~~~~~~~~~~~~~

Introduction

~~~~~~~~~~~~~

The Sea Islands are a chain of islands in the Atlantic Ocean off the East Coast of North America. These islands extend from northern Florida to the coasts of Georgia, South Carolina, North Carolina, and Virginia.

The Sea Islands are unique because they are the home of African Prisoners of the Race War (Gullah slaves) from West Africa, the Congo area and the African interior.

The origin of the work, "Gullah," is mixed and varied. "Gull" may mean God, and "ah" is a word placed before or after a root word. It usually refers to a blessing. This would mean that "Gullah" could be translated as "the blessing of God," or "the people blessed by God." Many African communal names refer to God or praise God. Further, the Gullah slaves have been related to the Gola and a mixture of central, southern Africans that had technology skills needed for slavery. They were shipped from many ports such as Sierra Leone ports. The Vai or Gala, or Gallians (another work for Vai) African ethnic group are the Gullah slaves.

The word Gullah is given to Africans that lived near the sea and/or rivers. These Gullah slaves are in areas that includes Tidewater, Virginia, parts of the Chesapeake Bay, and extends 50 miles inland, continuing down to east coast to Mayport, Florida. The words Gullah, Trinidadian, Jamaican, Puerto Rican, Latino, Creole, identify Africans slaves as separate ethnic groups. These words were created by Whites to keep Africans mistrustful of each other and divided from each other. White people caused further division of African people by classifying light-skinned Africans and Africans with Caucasoid physical features or lifestyles are better off (superior) and beautiful and dark skin Africans are classified as ugly. Historically, Gullah people were captured from many areas of Africa especially the Rice Coast of West Africa. The technologically advanced Africans had many counterattacks (so-called rebellions) on the continent of

11

Africa, on ships and plantations. They were forcefully brought to the Sea Islands because the Europeans were without human resources, (labor, technology), and natural resources (land). White people needed the African Slaves technology to build their stolen wealth, and stolen land (American colonies).

The Gullah captives possessed skills (technology) in agriculture, science, military science, tool making, bookkeeping, sailors, cabinet making, soldiers, furniture making, construction, banking, government, teaching, and most of all, they had over 1 million years in the most developed civilization in the world—that of Africa. It is the African technology that produced European and European-American stolen wealth. The Europeans maintain their stolen wealth by owning and controlling the United States of America through the Federal Reserve. The Internal Revenue Services illegally collects taxes and gives the money to a privately-owned Banksters (Bank gangster money thieves) business called the Federal Reserve. This foreign Banksters company gained its power from slavery and control the value (price) of money in order to control the American economy and military, and thereby, European control of America and Africa. This could not have been done without the money gained from African slavery (European type of welfare) and exploiting poor Whites and wage slaves.

During colonial times, the European-Americans tried unsuccessfully to profit from southern natural resources (land). However, without the human resource of African people, and African technology, they failed. American Indians and White indentured workers were enslaved. Slavery was unproductive because the Whites and Native Americans had labor but lacked technology skills for building the infrastructure and agriculture and fishing techniques. Finally, the Europeans used the slave Trans-Pacific and Trans-Atlantic slave routes and slavery developed by the Asians, East Indians, Chinese, and Arab enslavers. This gave them success with African slave labor and technology. Thus, African chattel slavery depopulated Africa, caused massive refugee immigration which forced African countries to weaken. This caused African tribes that never had contact with each other to begin to have clashes over food crops, food animals, and territories. Many African crops were burnt by Whites. And they murdered skilled black engineers, teachers, carpenters, plumbers, sailors, babysitters, builders, doctors, midwives, schools, scientist, and artist. Many buildings, factories, ships, schools, farms, hospitals, and homes were destroyed by the Asian, Arabs, Persians, Chinese, Europeans etc. The rape of Africa for natural resources (land, gold, diamonds, wood etc.) and human resources, and the transportation of Black people with the skills to the American coast inadvertently created a geographical area in the Sea Islands, uniquely African.

The Gullah captives produced high profits for the Europeans. These sea island slaves were not brought from the American mainland slave breeders or mainland plantations or mixing ports. Gullahs were brought directly from Africa to the islands. The isolation on island allowed the maximum labor output on the islands and were not allowed to mix with other Blacks. The Gullah were prized possessions as "slaves" and sold at higher prices than other African slaves. This justified breeding sea island black only with sea island blacks. During enslavement, the Gullah were left on the Sea Islands to themselves except for overseers (White supervisors). The planters (plantation owners) lived on the mainland or northern cities. They made periodic visits to the islands to check on crop production and on the "seasonin" and breeding of the Gullah slave livestock (stocks) and bondage (bond in chains).

The isolation of the Gullah from mainland Whites and other Africans allowed the Gullah to maintain African culture. Gullah is more than an ethnic group of people that have the same rituals, ceremonies, history and experience in common but also act as form of storage of African history. Gullah history helps Black people solve current problems (i.e., economic, social, spiritual, and military) and to transmits and translate African culture. The high concentration of African people bought directly from Africa allowed a Gullah Community to form (an Afrocentric cultural entity within a European-American cultural context). Further, after the end of the European intertribal war (Civil War), the Gullah remained isolated from whites from 1861 to 1930. During 1930, bridges were built that connected the mainland to the islands. Since that time, Whites have continued to steal and buy land and turn the island into a tourist attraction and residence for Whites. These historical, ancestral and sea lands are losing their African cultural footprint.

The Gullah African American people have been noted for their speech patterns and English language usage. The Gullah "accent" is more than a West African and Congo language accent on English. Oddly enough, English is basically a degenerate mixture of German words and bastardized Latinized African words. English is not actually a distinct language. Gullah is an African language that uses African word order and conceptual meanings. In other words, the Gullah language is uniquely an African language, with English words added to it. In addition to the Gullah language, the Gullah people have a lifestyle and a heritage that has left its mark on American and world history.

Word order determines language. If you use Spanish words with an African word order and concepts it transmits the African way of thinking. Therefore, the Africanism in the African word order can not be translated as if it were Spanish grammar. Many ideas and concepts can not be translated from one language to another language. And, many African ideas and concepts can not be translated by using the English language grammar standards. Consequently, you must use Africanism (ideas, concepts) to understand Gullah word order ideas and concepts. An African speaking French, Spanish, or English if using an African word order, colloquial expressions and concepts is speaking as if they are using Swahili, Wolof, Twi, etc. grammar. Therefore, Gullah is a foreign language from an African language group.

Where Gullahs Come From

The majority of the African Americans (all Gullahs) came from the urban cities of West Africa. The urban cities' area covered 2.5 million square miles, which is the size of the United States. West Africa is an area of low country grassland (three-fourths of it) and not a desert or jungle area. The area is similar to the Sea Island and East coastal states of Southern America. The 200 to 300 cities of urban Africa had walls built around them. Within the major walls would be other circular walls with distances of up to three-quarter miles apart. Some of the large cities would cover an area the size of Texas with a single castle covering 640 acres.

The walls were up to 100 miles in circular length, 40 to 50 feet in height and 30 feet wide. Within the city there were farms, schools, factories, herb farms, lakes, storage buildings, and stables of over 1,000 horses, donkeys, or camels. An African walled city would be divided into over 120 wards or districts with each district having a mayor. Small towns and surrounding suburban areas or villages were part of the large city. The cities had paved streets up to 300 feet wide, two-story buildings with glass windows, stores, colleges, churches, and no police and no jails. There are no words for jail or orphans in African language because there were no jails or orphans. African cities were built to reflect the laws of Maat (truth, justice, balance, harmony, reciprocity, propriety) God, nature, and culture (see the book Pher Ankh by L. Afrika). The family was the foundation of African cultures and cities and served to holistically (spirit, emotion, mind, and body) influence an individual's Maat behavior and thus control the cities.

The large urban metropolitan cities were part of many African countries such as Sierra Leone, Benin, Ghana, Liberia, and Ivory Cost. Many smaller cities such as Jenne, Kumasi, Segu and Ife plus towns and villages were part of great empires such as Mali, Bornu, Kong,

Mossi, and Asante empires. These cities date back as far as 1 A.D. Mandara, 9 A.D.; Kanem-Bornu, 1100 Katsina, 1350 Gobir, and up to the 18th century. They had many industries in shipbuilding, metal, textile, commerce, literature, colleges, medicine, and imported and exported to Asia, India, China, Arabic Countries, and the Americas. Some cities had populations of 400,000 people with over 70,000 people a day commuting to work in craft and technical factories, schools, bookkeeping, language translators, or to agricultural fields of millet, wheat, corn, plantain, rice, and cotton.

The cities were invaded Hyksos, Persians, Syrians, East Indians, Chinese, Arabs, Greeks, Romans, and lastly by the Europeans in the 13th century. Historically, the ancient Greeks never claimed to be a part of Europe. Ancient Greeks and Romans said the Europeans were barbarians, savages, infidels, brutes (brits, Britain's) and cave dwellers. When the Europeans captured Greece, they claimed Creek culture as the root of their own culture. Europe came into existence after the fall of the Mediterranean countries of Greece and Rome. Europeans used biological warfare (diseases), chemicals (drugs and alcohol), spiritual (Africans forced to adopt European religions and call their own Maat spirituality (pagan), psychological (made to feel inferior), and military warfare (guns, rockets, hot canon balls, bombs) to defeat Africa. It is estimated that 500,000,000 Africans and African Americans (included Gullahs) were murdered by the invasions, colonialism and slavery business.

There were Gullah Africans on many sea islands and mainlands near water that were a prized commodity in the slavery business and sort after by other races. It seems to be that Africa's human resource (technology, science, skills, etc.) and natural resources (gold, trees, silver, farmland) is what everybody (Arabs, East Indians, Chinese, Europeans) wanted and nobody wanted to pay for = slavery, exploitation of land.

The exploitation, enslavement and invasion of Africa started on the Pacific Ocean side of the Africa's west coast and North Africa. African people were stolen from Madagascar Island, Mozambique, Sofala, Mombasa, Mogadishu, Ethiopia, Nile River basin, Red Sea ports (by Cairo), Morocco, Yemen, Arabia Sea Slave port of Muscat, Persia Gulf slave port of Ormuz, Malabar, and enslaved on islands in the Indian Ocean, Ceylon Island, Bay of Bengal ports, Ganges River ports of China, Malacca, Sumatra, Java, Bornea, Celebes, and China's slave ports of Canton and Hangchow.

There were African slaves in India, China, Pakistan, Tibet, France, England, Portugal, Prussia, Spain etc. In 1417 Chinese junk ships were in East African ports involved in slavery. African slaves were in India and Asia Minor. The slaves were used on rice, sugar, and cotton plantations. Arabs sold African slaves in India and China. Literatures of India references sugar plantations such as the Ramayana sugar factory and the maxims of Buddhist philosophy mention the slave trade. The Arab slave trade provided slaves for sugar plantations of Egypt, Crete Greece, Syria, Sicily, Cyprus, Spain, Malta, and Rhodes.

China's Tang Dynasty and Qin King (221 BC) unified China which increased the invasion of Africa for slaves. Incidentally, there is a large Black African population in India and China today because of the slave trade. Tang Dynasty (618-907), Song Dynasty (960-1275) and Ming Dynasty (1368-1644) were involved in the Black African slave trade. The Chinese called the Black slaves Kunlun which means Dark Devils. China's Admiral Zneng (1500) was doing slave trading in southeast Africa. When Genghis Kahn's Mongul Empire unified Chinese tribes that traded on the Silk road. It escalated the slave trade. The Monguls ruled China, Korea, and Euro-Asia. The Chinese and East Indians involvement in slavery spreaded African peoples and Gullah peoples over Europe and Asia. The Orientals were in the slave trade before the Europeans got involved. The infrastructure and market for slavery and use of world maps made slavery an established business. White people took it over because they were a superior military power.

The massive African deaths during the 2,000 years of Arab slavery and the Arab Trans- Pacific slave trade in North and East Africa to China and India have vague numerical figures of the slave trade. The over 1,000 years of the China, India, and Asians Trans-Pacific slave trade did not record deaths of commodities called slaves.

The White military powerful tribes entered the Trans-Atlantic Slave trade after the slave trade routes, and trade methods were established. The majority of slave deaths occurred with European slave trades in South America, and Caribbean. Slave deaths estimates are based primarily on conjectures of the European North American slave trade. Those deaths estimates did not include those Africans that died during slave capture invasions, the slaves that walked from the interior to the coastal ports, slave suicides, harsh work, deaths, European cause deaths, diseases, during slave ocean transportation deaths, castration of slave men that served as guards, teachers, and bookkeepers, medical experiments, Slaves caused by White cannibalism on slave ships due to food shortage, and the African soldiers, and sailors that died fighting against slavery.

Keep in mind that at the time of slavery Europe, Arabia, Asia, and China were not formally constituted as countries. They were illiterate unorganized tribes and gangs. These barbaric primitive military powerful tribes fought each other on land and sea for the African slaves. European tribes were illiterate and did not keep accurate records unless they were forced to pay tax money or pay with goods or slaves to another tribe. Therefore, the 200,000,000 slave deaths are a modest conjecture made from North American Slave records.

Gullah Language Path

The Gullah language path follows the slave trade route. They were African prisoners of war because African countries fought for over 2,000 years to stop the Arabs, East Indians, China, and then fought 400 years to stop the tribes of European invasion armies.

The cargo ships loaded with goods started in European countries, such as Ireland, England, France, Spain, Italy, and Portugal. Then they would go to Africa, the Canary Islands, Cape Verde, across the Atlantic Ocean to South America, Haiti, Barbados, Hispaniola, and Cuba. The slave trade route of the Gulf of Mexico, which included Louisiana and Alabama. From there, slave traders would go to the Bahamas and the Gullah slave-concentrated areas of the Sea Islands (Florida, Georgia, South and North Carolina, and Virginia), and then Bermuda.

Today, there is still a common linguistic connection with West Africans in the Caribbean, India, China, and from Louisiana to Charleston.

Gullah Medu Netcher

The ancient Africans originally came to the Americans around 5000 BC and brought with them plants, technology, culture, and language. The early American Quachita natives were probably from the Mali region of Africa and related to the Mende. They taught the Native Americans technology, military science, music, words, culture, religion, and influenced the clothing styles of the ancient Natives. Many of the ancient African contributions are erroneously attributed to the Native Americans. For example, the African Moors (Ethiopians) introduced music to Spain. Consequently, African harmonies and rhythms are erroneously called Latin music. The Quachitas lived on 3 million acres of land that covered part of Texas, Mississippi, Louisiana, Arkansas, and Oklahoma. The Jamassi (Yamesee) African people lived in the Carolinas Sea Islands, Florida, and Georgia. The so-called Carib ancient Africans lived in Mexico (included California), the Caribbean Islands, and South and Central Americas. These ancient Africans traded goods with Africans on the continent of Africa before Europeans discovered (invaded) America. It is erroneously assumed that the ancient Africans style of clothing, words, and music is Native American. The Europeans called these Africans very dark skinned Indians and named them Black Foot, Tar Heels, Brass Ankles, etc. These ancient Africans constructed Pyramids, High-rise apartments buildings, and cities with African technology.

Ancient Africans born in America and those that came to America before Columbus, introduced African words. For example, the African Medu Netcher words Neb = Lord, Ra = God, which combines to form the work "Metro (Ruling Place)"; Mat (Maat) = Justice; Ur (or) = order which combines to form the English work "Mayor" = Keeper of Order; Sala = garden which mistranslates to the English word "salad"; the nine Fauts (Gods) who decided upon who is to blame for wrong behavior, which translates to the English work, "Fault"; A-Meru (Amir)= Leader, Kas = Life, combines to form "America" (Leader of Life).

The primitive Europeans tribes (so-called countries), arrived in Africa were illiterate with a limited vocabulary of very few words. Their few "grunt" sounding words reflected their Cave civilization and Ice Age civilization. Caucasian Cave (Troglodytes) origins are written in Plato's "Allegory of the Cave" (514-520) in his book the Republic (book 7 and 8). He describes the Caucasian emotions and mentality are from the distorted shadows of reality. Ancient Greece's Aristotle student Theophrastus play "The Characters" (319 B.C) describes the 30 negative traits of the Caucasian personalities. Sigmund Freud subconsciously refers to cave civilization's impact on White people's emotions and mentality as the female's womb as a cave. The cave civilization helped to create their personality. Charles Darwin suggest that the animal brain is the cave mind. The Post Traumatic Cave Disorder still has an effect on language. Caucasians were "Hun" = without spirit or food and called themselves Hungry, Hungarians, Hunters, etc. They had trouble pronouncing the cluster vowels and the "L" and "r" of African language. This lead to mispronunciations and mistranslations. In other words, the Caucasians speak a primitive bastardized Latin. The so-called Africanism in the Gullah language is incorrect. There is Africanism in European language. Primitive Europeans stole African words, mispronounced them, Latinized them, and called them Latin words. English, as well as American English, is a Saxon dialect consisting of combinations of German words mixed with Latinized African words. English is not by definition a language, but a form of bastardized African words. Europeans have a criminal relationship with Africans and have stolen African words, culture, resources, music, technology and African people (slaves). In their attempt to use their Left Mind, (Rational, Logical, and Intellectual part of the brain) they have failed to construct a true democracy, ecology, culture, and language. For example, they constructed a European school system that fails African people, agriculture that chemically pollutes the soil, water, air, and food, all of which causes diseases. They have created an economic system that exploits the poor, creates poverty, and bail outs for the rich and a legal system that punishes the innocent. The USA has the largest prison population and women's prison in the world. This English language has over 400 negative connotations for the word Black (Black Monday, Black Mail, Black Humor, Black Lie, Blacken Your Name, Black Cat, Black Ball, Black List, etc.) this causes Black people to be inferiorized by the English language.

Medu Netcher (Egyptian hieroglyphic language) words are the original words of the African peoples' languages. The Caucasian historians deny the Medu Netcher language and the Congolese (Sudan area) words in Gullah and associate Gullah language as a slang used by Black people.

Sea Island Indians

The territory called Carolinas was called Chicora and America was called Turtle Island by the Native Americans. Africa was called Ake Bu Lan by its natives. The Indians were misused, mistreated, abused, exploited, and denied use of their own land. Many of them moved away from the European invaders in mass immigration and became refugees in their own land. The natives were culturally disenfranchised. Some Natives lived near Europeans were raped by White invadors and became racially mixed (African Indians, Afro-American Indians, and Euro-Indians). The Catawba natives lived on the pitiful wilderness ghetto called a reservation, in York County, South Carolina. In the 1930 census, Croatians (also called Turks, Brass Ankles, and Redbones) were identified. The early African voyages to America before the invasion of Columbus caused an European cultural influence in the cultures of the Creeks, Cherokee, Chickasaw, and Choctaw. The Indian inhabitants of the islands such as the Gaule, Cusabo, and then the Yemasses were murdered, scalped, raped, domesticated, or sold as slaves. Yemasses (Yamesse) along with other Black Native Americans were described as having thick lips, woolly hair, and black skin by early European explorers (invaders). Early Europeans only knew of one group of Black people, those that lived in India (Untouchables). Therefore, they called the Africans—Indians. The Sea Island Indians became a part of Gullah Island culture and history. The Europeans that the Indians, Africans, and Gullahs Africans met by white people that did not bathe, use deodorant, had disease, ticks, fleas, rotten teeth, men didn't shave, women did not shave legs, armpits, arms, and had matted hair, bad breathe, could not read or write, wore rags, animal skins and fur, were superstitious, had venereal diseases and believed themselves superior to Black people and Indians. The State of Georgia was created as a European prisoner colony (prison state) by King George. He named the state of Georgia after himself. European tribal gangs of countries used American (and the Sea Islands) as dumpsites (social trash can) for cargoes of social undesirables such as criminals, beggars, thieves, rapist, the handicap, cripples, the blind, orphans, whores, the homeless, welfare recipients, the diseased, and the mentally ill. They loaded the undesirables on ships called "The Ship of Fools" and sent them to America. Additionally, European-Americans criminals and runaway White indentured slaves came to the islands, such as Aaron Burr on St. Simeon's Island after killing Alexander Hamilton. Edgar Allen Poe was inspired to write, "The Golden Bug" while on Sullivan's Island, near Charleston. The Indians and Africans were forcefully subjected to the worst of European society. They have survived and have fought against the European's invaders.

Currently, the United States government refuses to recognize the Edisto Indians as Native Americans and will not register them with the Bureau of Indian Affairs. They are not allowed to practice many parts of their culture. Currently, America's Inca Indians and so-called Mexicans are called refugees. They are not allowed to freely travel in their original Native American lands of California, Arizona, Texas, Georgia etc. The U.S.A claims they are illegally crossing the borders in California and Texas. The natives are hunted, worked as wage slaves, prostitutes, murdered and raped and put in jail for travelling in their own lands.

Gullah Warrior from runaway slave communities

attacked whites.

Amazing Facts About the Gullah People and the Sea Islands

1. 1461 – Sir Henry, the Navigator of France usurped the African ship building techniques, designs, and sailing methods. He used the sale of slaves to finance construction of the new designed ships that could come close to shore, move fast, and carry large slave cargoes (300-400). These ships ignited the slave trade, which eventually brought Africans such as the Gullahs to America.

2. 1477 – Christopher Columbus (a Jew raised in Italy, hired by Spain) came to Hispaniola (Cuba) then to the Sea Islands. He never came to North America. He was a Portuguese Jew involved in the slave trade for over 10 years before he came to Hispanola. At age 14 he started working in the slave trade. Columbus was responsible for the murders of thousands of Black people, Carib Indians and Native Americans. He did not discover Hispaniola, (Cuba, Haiti, etc.). In recorded history in 1296, Mansu Musa III of Africa had a map of the round world and was sending ships back and forth to the Americas before Columbus invasions.

3. 1500 – The concept of "Wonderland" brought to America by the Gullahs. An African concept "Gondwanland" (English, wonderland) is the belief of paradise on Earth. It is the name given to the belief of a single land mass (World Island) that all continents were believed to be a part of before they drifted apart creating Africa, the Americas, etc. The rites of passage fairy tale, "Alice in Wonderland" alludes to Gondwanland.

4. 1500 – The Gullahs were estimated to live to be 140 to 200 years of age.

5. 1500 – The beginning of the deliberate murder of people in the African Babysitting Art (Kindezi), similar to preschools and included teaching. The Babysitters (Ndezi) included the youth and elderly. They freely babysat between different African ethnic groups, families and tribes and helped to maintain cultural harmony amongst African ethnic groups, Gullahs, and other Africans.

6. 1500 – The European ganus (gangs) tribal ethnic groups evolved to become the tribal feudal caste system. The landless gangs' labor was exploited by the ruling landlords. The feudal Kings exploited the White poor landless peasants. They were forced to work without pay. Peasants revolted and cause economic problems for the rich self proclaimed kings, so the kings bought African slaves to solve their money problems. The African chattel slaves were put in work gangs pattern after the feudal gangs of the caste system. They worked in the house, fields, were basket makers, bookkeepers, sailors, translators, breeders, and skilled crafts. African slaves were denied the right to use their culture, language, food, religion, and clothes. They were also classified as animals, used as pets for children, and branded with the approval of all European religions. However, the Gullah isolated on islands did use African rituals and ceremonies.

7. 1500 – The use of the custom of leaving glasses, mirrors, dishes, and shining objects on graves is an African ritual and ceremony custom used to help the deceased travel to the heavens. This is

similar to artifacts, furniture, clothes, jewelry, food, and books found in Egyptian Pyramids. Gullahs continued the custom of leaving a meal (dinner) on the grave or the porch for the deceased. The ancient Southern Africans practice the same custom and place artifacts in the wooden Pyramids.

Original Indigenous Chief John Horse
Led attacks on U.S. troops, Black Seminole
Indians (Africans), and Gullah Runaways

8. 1500 – The "Chain of Death" or the "Chains of Bad Luck" ritual was used by the Gullahs. Gullahs would break glasses, mirrors, bottles, or dishes in order to stop a series (chain) of bad luck events or death. Europeans, typically break a martini glass in a fireplace to break the chain of bad luck.

Ancient Egyptian mural form Beni Hasan
(Martial Arts)

9. 1500 – Many of the African military scientists (warriors) that fought counterattacks (rebellions, revolts, etc.) against the Europeans were called "The People Who Could Fly." This referred to African Martial Artist Capoeira (a type of Judo, Kung Fu), who seem to fly high in the air in order to do kicks. The Europeans had never seen Martial Arts nor could they do it. Martial Artists skills were brought to America by Africans.

10. 1510 – First contemporary West Africans in America came to the Sea Islands. They traveled to St. Augustine, Florida with Ponce De Leon. These were free Africans that did not experienced slavery.

11. 1520 –The sea islands were named after a saint. The invader Gordillo landed at Coffin's Point on Good Friday and named the grouping of islands, St. Helena. It included the areas from Edisto, South Carolina to Savannah, Georgia.

12. 1520 –Native Americans kidnaped. The invader Gordillo kidnaped Yemassees and attempted to

take them to Europe. His ship sank and all the Yemassees he had stolen drowned.

13. 1520 – Lucas Vasquez de Ayllon came to the Sea Islands in search of Gullahs who were skilled in mining and agriculture. He took them to Santo Domingo, South America.

14. 1523 – An outbreak of a major contagious virus disease. More than 500 Africans died of diseases they caught from White people. This epidemic happened at Cape Fear, North Carolina.

15. 1526 – Pigs brought to America arrived at Parris Island with De Ayllon...

16. 1526 –African Americans born on St. Catherine's Island organized a Gullah rebellion that led to their liberation and freedom on St. Catherine's Island.

17. 1526 –A major American city abandoned was Winyah Bay City on St. Helena Island. The White people could not tolerate the humidity, mosquitos, and they feared slave raids and abandoned the city.

18. 1562 – Captain John Hawkins (1532-1595) captured 300 Africans from Sierra Leone. Some were able to return to their homeland.

19. 1563 – Ships built in America, by skilled ship building African slaves that designed the African ship type. The Yemassees helped Nicholas Barro's men design and build African type ships.

20. 1563 – Cannibalism on St. Helena Island. Jean Ribaut, a Frenchman, and his crew ran out of food

and began eating each others human flesh. The African Egyptians of the 9th Dynasty recorded White peoples cannibalism in Europe in 3000 B.C.

21. 1565 – The use of African "Pit and Pebble" games in America. The European games of baseball, cricket, volleyball, marbles, football, tennis, soccer, pocket pool, basketball, and golf (Gentle Only Ladies Forbidden anagram) are all forms of the ancient African Pit and Pebble games that the Gullah and ancient Africans played.

22. 1566 – Fort San Felipe was built on Parris Island by African slaves owned by the Spanish.

23. 1566 – The White enslavers and colonizers forcefully taught the Catholic, Jewish, and Muslim religion to slaves and Native Americans on Parris Island. Gullah slaves were herded and whipped to church like cattle. They had to deny their own spirituality and call it evil, pagan, and ungodly.

24. 1587 Spain purchased Native American captives ("slaves"). Later, in history, Native Americans would own African slave plantations.

25. 1600 –Christmas holidays. A few Gullah captives were allowed to sell goods, seafood, and their labor to others. They could keep the earnings and had to pay a tax on earnings. The slave master introduced drinking alcohol, and smoking marijuana as a way to celebrate on weekends and holidays. The Gullahs performed the "Jehuti" ritual whereby the Elder slaves used a mock Scepter (cane), Eye of Heru Hat (Raccoon Hat) and Ankh (Christian Cross) and would lead groups of slaves in a ritual march to the slave master's Big House to collect coins in a cup from each white

person in the house. The coins symbolized righteous deeds that the person had done in life. The coins also symbolized amount of good deeds needed to buy their way into heaven on the day of judgment of the soul. White people would give slaves to each other as Christmas presents. Slave children were gifts given to White children to keep as pets.

26. 1600 – "Silly" stories told by the Gullas. "Jelle" tales were told by the Sierra Leone Gullahs. These were tall tales that required improvising and much acting out and pantomime. Telling these Tales was called "acting silly" (Jelle) by White enslavers.

27. 1600 – Galee (African head wrap) used by Gullah women. Later they straightened their hair by using heated forks. Men used axle grease to make their hair limp or cut their kinky hair very short so that their hair would not show curliness (kinky) and shaved a part in the hair so that it would resemble the part in white male's hair (straight and limp).

28. 1600 – "Cowboys," were the Gullah captives from Ghana and from the Gambia River (Senegal), They were brought to the Sea Islands because they were expert horsemen and herdsmen. The Black men would go in the woods to get stray and run away cows and were called cowboys. Black men were called "boys" and Black women were called "gals"

29. 1600 – Use of Brer Rabbit, Bugs Bunny and Mickey Mouse stories. These were trickster tales based on an intelligent hero that outwitted the forces of the unknown, evil, solve problems, escaped bad

situations, and had supernatural powers. The stories are versions of the African Ashanti spider tales. The African Aesop Fables stories were given a negative name of "Cock and Bull stories". "Cock" refers to the Maat African bird of Morality. "Bull" was decrees of morality in the Catholic Pope's newsletter. The protesters (Protestant) view the Pope as immoral to make judgment on their version of Christianity. The protesters called his orders "Cock and Bull" immoral stories.

30. 1600 – Bricklayers and Masons technology of Gullahs was used to construct forts, factories, homes, etc.. Spain learned of this skill from the Moors and West Africans during the time Mansa Musa made his pilgrimage to Mecca (1324-1325). Spain would later pay high prices for skilled Gullah captives.

31. 1600 – Slaves were given seven years to live! Portuguese enslavers predicted that the slaves (Gullah captives) would live seven years and then drop dead from physical exhaustion. It was feared that if slavery did not end or if the slaves did not die from exhaustion, then they would be a majority in America.

32. 1600 – The Sea Islands maintain the African Secret Societies schools of Poro for men and Sande for women. These were called "Bush" schools that provided cultural reinforcement, rituals, and ceremonies. They learned the "Rites of Passage" which are classes in Maat behavior for marriage, parenting, adulthood, village, spirituality, economics, problem solving, diet, herbs, along with military tactics and how to revolt.

33. 1600 – Africans were branded with hot irons that cooked the flesh. These brands were called "Country Scars" or "Country Marks" and helped to identify the owner of the slave and helped identity freedom-seeking runaway slaves.

34. 1600 – Gullahs used the "Chevron" to rank position. The police and military use chevron stripes indicating the status of the soldiers ranking. Secret societies of Poro and Sande used chevron-type markings during initiation rituals to show step-by-step progressions. These marks could be cut on the skin of the cheeks of the face, arm or forehead.

35. 1600 – Gullahs were purchased for technological skills as metal workers, agricultural experts, barrel makers, bricklayers, swamp fishermen, cotton quilt weavers (quilted without stitching), herdsmen, deep sea divers, herbalists, chemists, bookkeepers, sailors, soldiers, teachers, translators, breeders, prostitutes, etc..

36. 1600 (circa) –Nondenominational church established by the Gullahs called the Praise House. Praise Houses were found on every plantation in the Sea Islands. Slaves in the house would sing and dance in a circle with a mediation trance called "Ring Shout." African dances copied by Europeans are Quizomba (Samba), Tangana (Tango), Charleston, Boogie Woogie, Rhumba, etc. Jazz dancing is a dance performed to the African music, called Jazz. Jazz is a negative term. Caucasians negatively called it "Jackass Music," which eventually became the word, Jazz. A similar type word is picnic, which originally meant ("Pick a Nigger") and lynch him. White people would bring families, food, and children,

put table clothes on the ground, sing, dance, pray, and drink alcohol while watching a lynching.

37. 1600 (circa) – Many exceptionally physically built or intelligent or skilled Gullahs and other slaves were sold to slave breeding farms in Virginia, Maryland, and Kentucky. These same states have switched to breeding horses for races. Some slaves were too crippled, damaged, diseased, or too old to do harsh work. They were sold at reduced rates at Refuse (Trash) Sales or Scramble Sales (Blue Light). Mr. J. Marion Sims, M.D. (Father of gynecology), bought such female slaves to practice operations (i.e., fistula, hysterectomies). Many African ladies died because he experimented on them without drugs, or sanitation. He addicted women to heroin, and sexually abused them. Slave children were trained to forcefully herd, whip, and drive cattle (50% of cowboys were black) and women to cane/cotton fields, church, whore houses and bargain refuse (damage slaves) Slave auction. Breastfeeding women were herded by children to the edge of working fields to nurse the babies.

38. 1600 –African chants used in America (later called Gospel) were used by Gullahs. These were used at weddings, on holidays, at funerals, births, and at many other ceremonies. "Boogie Woogie" a negative name given to African dance music. "Boogie" mythological witch/devil. "Woogie" richochet or syncopated or incomplete raggardly off rhythm music beat Boogie Woogie = Devils Dance.
Those White people that thought niggers should be free were "Devils Advocate". During canonization (voting) ceremony for a new cardinal a debate (discussion) on his approval or

disapproval had speakers for approval as "God's Advocate" and speakers for disapproval or "Devils Advocate".

39. 1600 – Gullah workers had skills in complex irrigation systems using dams, ditches, and slues. These Africans were purchased directly from Africa's "Rice Coast" or the "Windward Coast" (the areas of Senegals, Sierra Leone, and Liberia) and sold to Sea Island plantations.

40. 1600 (circa) –African American and Gullah communities used "The Silent Trade". Buying and Selling based on the honesty of the buyer and seller. For example, an owner would leave his store and leave items for sale. The customer could come at any time, pick up the goods and leave payment. The goods and money were never stolen. "The Silent Trade" was used in Mali, Songhay, Ghana, Sudan, Ethiopia, etc.

41. 1600 (circa) – "Basket Names" were given by Elders, to infants and children that identified their Ancestral Spirit, Mission in Life, etc. A "Nickname" is given later in a person's life by a friend or relative and can be based on personality characteristics.

42. 1600 – Palm leaf brooms were made by Gullahs. These were of African origin as is the art of basket weaving. The brooms were symbols of the cleanliness of God and used to keep away evil spirits. Palm leaves were walked upon during fertility rituals to purify the person for conception.

43. 1600 – The word "Nigger" was used in reference to slaves and Gullahs captured from the Niger Bend land area or the Niger River area of Africa.

These slaves were called Nigers which was pronounce "Niggers" by White People.

44. 1600 – Largest tabby fort in America, Fort Frederick, was located off the shore of the Broad River on a peninsula between Beaufort and Port Royal. It was built by slaves.

45. 1626 – Gullah and other slave African captives They were Prisoners of War that were captured during White peoples invasion. They were brought to Algoinga Island (Native American name for Sea Islands) off the coast of Turtle Island (Native American name for the continent of America).

46. 1640 –The White slavery business had African slave sailors that used navigation and astrological skills learnt in Africa. The "Drinking Gourd," (called the "Big Dipper" by Whites) was referred to when crossing the Atlantic Ocean.

47. 1670 – One of the first cities in America was established at Port Royal by the Spaniards. The site for this city was later moved because of attacks by the Portuguese, French, Russians, and English. It is now called Charleston, South Carolina.

48. 1670 – Planters using Gambian herdsmen (cowboys) because they were cheap and free labor. It was said to raise cattle on the Sea Islands is as cheap as raising chickens.

49. 1670 – Female doctors in America were Gullah women, so-called herbalists. They were Priestesses, Warriors, and Midwives and often organized slave rebellions.

50. 1670 – Native Americans were exported as slaves. Mulattos were half-breed mixtures of West Africans and Indians were sold at a higher price. There were many slave breeders that practice mixing races Africans with Natives, African mule people (mulattos) with White people then that mulatto was mixed with natives. There were a variety of racial mixtures, studs and breeder slaves for sale.

51. 1670 – White Peoples Diseases were used as weapons to destroy Indians. The death rate of Indians (Coosaw, Creek, Yemassee, Cherokee) increased due to contact with diseased Sea Island Europeans.

52. 1671 – Indian slaves bought with Gullah slave labor. The price for Indian slaves was paid with rice, turpentine, deer skins, pine, and pigs.

53. 1672 – New Yorkers moved to Sea Islands to get in on financial profits of Gullah slavery. Dutch settlers from Harlem New York came to the Carolinas. In the beginning a Black male slave sold for 4 horses due to livestock competitors the price was reduced to 1 horse for 1 male and 4 pigs for 1 female. The Atlantic slave trade sold 6 men to 1 woman. The Trans Pacific Slave Trade sold 4 women to each 1 male. Usually, the male was castrated and used to guard harems, or as translators, bookkeepers, teachers, or slave soldiers and sailors.

54. 1680 – Madagascar Africans taught Dr. Henry of Beaufort agricultural knowledge. He subsequently utilized West Africans to start rice farming in Beaufort County.

55. 1683 –White slave rustlers hid on the sea island. Sea rustlers (pirates) increased stealing slaves in Carolina and made such profits from stealing West African slaves that they were able to retire in Carolina.

56. 1700 – The newspaper, Carolina Gazette, reported that the General Assembly bought an African-trained Gullah doctor (herbalist), named Caesar because he cured diseases.   Later, it became illegal for White doctors and drug stores to use African-trained doctors in their practice. However, many doctors own African doctors up until the Civil War.

57. 1700 – On-the-job injuries were recorded. Planters allowed work-related injuries to go untreated. Female workers suffered from "Craw-Craw," which was itching pus filled bumps. "Craw-Yaws" was a painful infection of the palms and soles caused by standing without shoes in plantation fields, and hand injuries from picking cotton cause palm sores.

58. 1700 – Usage of African recipes: "Jollof rice," a red rice, okra, fish gumbo; "Agidi," a boiled corn pasta, and "Fufu," a wheat porridge.

59. 1700 – Gullahs would paint the doors on their homes royal blue as found in the Pyramid of Giza. Blue symbolized the highest order of wisdom and the worship of God. George Washington Carver successfully duplicated the color while White people's computers and chemical analysis could not.

60. 1700 – Positive-thinking usage. "The Root Doctor" or "Doctor Buzzard" used the power of positive thinking concept in order to help a person to believe in the things that they desired, i.e. escaping slavery, avoiding bad luck, illness or getting money. It was believed that the doctor could stop buzzards from waiting for you to die. In modern times, this concept was popularized by Norman Vincent Peale.

61. 1700 – More than 200 Black soldiers from Haiti were sent by Toussaint L'Ouverture to help liberate African American slaves, Gullahs and ex-slaves. These black soldiers fought and then stayed in America and relocated in Nova Scotia. The ex-slave Toussaint lead the Haitian rebellion and defeated every European Army making Haiti the first slave liberated island and country.

62. 1700 – Captain Paul Coffee started a Back-to-Africa movement and shipped former slaves and free slaves back to Africa.

63. 1701 – Profits from Gullah enslavement were used by the East India Company to found Yale University in Connecticut.

64. 1702 – Sea Island Native American community stolen. The English, during Queen Anne's war, wanted more Native American workers (slaves), so they stole an entire Creek community.

65. 1702 – The French paid some Cherokees to murder Conchak Emika, a Choctaw. English, French, and Spanish tried to get Indians to fight on their sides by instigating wars between various Indian tribes and using espionage tactics (murdering and scalping Indians).

66. 1712 – "No knock" search and seizure law. Gullah and other slave homes were searched every 14 days during slavery and they were subjected to "Stop and Frisk" at anytime of day or night.

67. 1714 – Tea came to the Sea Islands' colonists. However, a favored drink was a popular Gullah mixture made from the stimulant cocoa bean (hot chocolate).

68. 1714 – High taxes charged for pure Africans in South Carolina due to the technology (skills) they possessed.

69. 1715 – The Yemassee War was fought. This was the war in which the combined Native American nations fought against the Whites. The Creeks, Choctaws, Catawbas and Yemassees joined forces and battled the Whites in the largest and most costly war in Carolina history. They continued their self-defense war from Edisto to St. Augustine until 1728. White people said they murdered so many Indians that they could walk across the Broad River without their feet getting wet.

70. 1717 – Colonials protest against England. Five-hundred seventy-three Negro slaves bought at 40 pounds (English money) tax per slave, caused the protest. Tax was high because slaves were skilled (Gullah).

71. 1718 – "Slave" rustling pirate was captured in the Sea Islands. Captain Teach or "Blackbeard" was the famous rustler.

72. 1730 - South Carolina Sea Island slave's expertise at rice cultivation created rice as a stable cash crop market. Many slaves died because of

malaria and infections from standing in swamp water. Other crops failed to be cash crops such as sugar cane, ginger, indigo, oranges, cotton, and silk.

73. 1732 – North Carolina was mostly established by Virginia tobacco businessmen and it served as a buffer state to protect the system of African American and African enslavement in South Carolina.

74. 1732 – King George issued a charter and sent England's mentally ill, thieves, prisoners, debtors, prostitutes, and homeless (social garbage) to a colony named Georgia. The state of Georgia was supposed to be a barrier that protected South Carolina and Spain's Florida. When Black Seminoles, Spaniards, and Indians started raiding Georgia. The King offered Blacks freedom if they would fight for England.

75. 1738 – The Cherokee smallpox epidemic. was often caused by Europeans giving Indians polluted water, rotten food, sexual diseases, fleas, and White diseases. The myth is smallpox toxic blankets was the cause. It can not be transmitted by blankets.

76. 1730 – The first freedom march in America. On September 9, 1739, Gullah people fought for their freedom during "Rebellions" in Charleston. There were many rebellions fought by Gullahs against enslavers, including the Stono River Revolt let by Cato. Some Gullahs had a non-violent slavery protest march to Georgia, North and South Carolina then to St Augustine Florida.

77. 1739 – Gullahs launched a series of attacks on planters that caused them to stop importing Africans for ten years. The planters feared that too many Africans that spoke the same language would be able to organize. They started breeding slaves to build a more docile group of blacks to help control the newly arrive African slaves.

78. 1740 – State highway patrol police force was unofficially organized to capture runaways and enforce the cruel Slave Codes. Today, they are called State Troopers.

79. 1742 – Gambian Africans in Gambia Africa attacked and destroyed the slaver ship, the "Mary Galley," which was destined for the Sea Islands of America.

80. 1745 – Gullahs harvested 104,680 barrels of rice, enough rice for American consumption and to export to the Mediterranean (yielded higher profits).

81. 1745 – White people invaded and violently took the land called Texas (stole) from Inca Indians called Native Americans. Many Gullahs that lived in Texas at that time were murdered by the White invasion.

82. 1748 – African chemistry teachers in America. Eliza Lucas Pickney was taught indigo extraction and color stabilization by Gullah textile craftsman from Africa.

83. 1750 – Bouncie Island slave shipyard, in the Sierra Leone River, was used by the English to build slave ships . The English sold slaves directly to

Charleston, and Sea Islands in South Carolina. These slaves were highly educated and skilled.

84. 1755 – South Carolina Provincial Legislature passed a law to keep free Blacks with advanced technological knowledge out of trades. The Blacks far outnumbered Whites in skilled trades during slavery and after the Civil War.

85. 1763 – The "Franciscan Mercenary and Missionary Technique" called the "Bible or the Bullet," was used on the Yemassee, natives, Gullah and murdered Inca Indians, in Texas, Mexican Natives of Americas in Arizona and California to steal their land called Mexico. Slave either accepted White peoples Bible or they would get the bullet (murdered).

86. 1764 – Free Gullah slave-labor gave England enormous wealth. All the cotton and other cash crops from the American colonies had to be shipped to the colonial powers, and then it was sold. This process allowed England, Spain, Portugal, Holland, Russia, and France to profit from slave-labor and build cities.

87. 1774 – Gullah slaves, no money down. Credit plan for purchase of slaves. After the American Revolution, the British continued to collect taxes in the American territory that they controlled. In an effort to sell Gullah and Indian slaves, the British sold slaves on credit and as lottery prizes. Sometimes they used payment plans of one-fourth to one-half down to sell slaves. This allow more wholesales of slaves to destroy the American Slave Markets wholesale and retail prices.

88. 1775 – Lacrosse was played in America. This game was introduced to White People in the Sea Island area by the Cherokee people.

89. 1776 – The original version of the Declaration of Independence gave slaves and ex-slaves their freedom. The Sea Islands' state representatives opposed this version, and had any references to freeing slaves omitted from the document.

90. 1781 –General Thomas Sumter during civil war sold slaves to pay his soldiers.

91. 1784 – Sea Islands' cotton increased the wealth of the South and saved the South from economic depression. Later in history, the hybridizer (plant breeder) and chemist George Washington Carver's products from the bean called the peanut caused the peanut and soy bean market to economically save the South from another depression.

92. 1788 – Gullahs and ex-slaves were the first African Americans to found a city in Africa. Freetown, Sierra Leone, the Capital, is the city they established. African American Gullah slave descendants of Sierra Leone moved back to that country .

93. 1790 – Gullah organization founded to maintain schools for children. The Brown Fellowship Society was founded in Charleston, South Carolina for educational matters affecting Black people.

94. 1795-1819 - Ft. Negro on the Apalchicola River sea island. The British lost two wars with the colonies because ex-slaves and runaways helped White People to fight the British.

95. 1800 – The largest U.S. export to the Mediterranean countries was Sea Islands' rice.

96. 1800 - Luis Avry, a Black pirate captain and his crew of runaway slaves lived on Amelia Sea Island near Jacksonville, Fl.

97. 1800 – Founding Fathers were salesman and user of drugs. George Washington had false wooden teeth that caused him pain, constantly and he constantly used opium, cocaine, alcohol, and smoked marijuana. He was the largest alcohol merchant in America. Benjamin Franklin was addicted to opium, and had a marijuana farm. Thomas Jefferson smoked marijuana, and was a marijuana farmer. Christopher Columbus used opium and would substitute nicotine when he could not get his drug.

98. 1800 – Mixed breed Blacks with Whites called Mule people or Mulatto Gullah's slavery businesses were ruined by Toussaint a Haitian. The Haitian Revolution, let by Toussaint L'Ouverture ruined the slavery business of Mulattoes. Mulatto ownership of other African Americans was created by Whites as a justification for the White slavery business. Many "free" African Americans bought the freedom of their parents and other relatives. They were technically classified as "slave owners" by White people.

99. 1800 – (circa) – The last shipment of Gullah captives (slaves) arrived in the Sea Islands. The ship landed at San Island, which is an island between Hardeeville and Ridgeland, South

Carolina. The bell of the ship is in the tower of Hardeeville Methodist Church.

100.   1800 – African Americans to demonstrate bravery in battle. "The Port Royal Experiment" was a test to show how bravely Blacks could defend White people in the Sea Islands.

101.   1800 – Black U.S. soldiers lynched in their uniforms by White Americans. After the Black Militia was organized to enforce marshal law and protect the North's capture of Southern territory, White vigilantes, militia, and mobs lynched many of Black Militia men.

102.   1800 – Race riots. Gullah homes were burned; people were murdered and girls and women raped because of the Black Militia's presence.

103.   1800 –African American State. During this time, 80 percent of the population of South Carolina was African American and consider a Black state.

104.   1800 – The highest point in South Carolina was given a name derived from the African language, (Sassa). The point is called Sassafras Mountain. Sassafras is also the name of an herb once used to treat syphilis.

105.   1800 – Gullah people would walk slowly and stop their funeral procession at the cemetery gate. This was done to gain spiritual permission to enter the spirit world (graveyard). Funeral procession travel slowly because of this practice.

106.   1800 – Totally independent African American communities were established. "Runaway Slave" communities were established by Gullahs from the Sea Island. They were found in northern Florida, lower Alabama, and Tennessee. The Spanish called these Africans "Seminoles," which is Spanish for "Cameroon," which is French for runaway slaves.

107.   1800 – Negro spiritual, "Swing Low, Sweet Harriet," sang to indicated escape via underground railroad. When Caucasians were around Gullah plans to escape were communicated in "time," "place," and "event" cryptic code of gospels songs. The gospel songs and words were often changed to "Swing Low, Sweet Chariot" when Whites were near. Today, it is sung as "Sing Low, Sweet Chariot."

108.   1800- Lloyds of London insured slaves and slave ships and their wealth.

109.   1800- Sea Island, Life Saving Service was renamed the Coast Guard. The Black Sailors rescued Whites Shipwrecked on E.S. Newman Ship.

110.   1800- Morris Code. The African drum rhythm language was stolen by a White man named Morris and renamed the Morris Code. The Morris Code is a type of Congo African drum electrical pulse rhythm (meter) and is used by telephones, television, computers, and radios. The electrical pulses are converted to words and/or pictures. Rhythm drum beat language was beat on the side of or wash tubs or a boat by Gullahs to communicate secret messages. Gullah fisherman used the Congo drum language to call

Dolphins and get them to herd fish to their nets. Gullah ladies would send messages by beating on wash tubs or scraping rhythm language on the clothes scrub hoards.

111.	1812 – Gullahs and runaway slaves were attacked by Andrew Jackson. General Jackson used the war of 1812 as an excuse to attack and murder the Gullahs in communities in Florida and lower Alabama.

112.	1812 – African myths, used by Gullahs, were called "tall tales" and some were published by David Crockett. The origins of these myths are found in the book, Coming Forth by Day, (so-called Egyptian Book of the Dead) written before 1500 B.C. and Aesop's fables.

113.	1812 – American marines were defeated by Gullahs and American Indians in Florida (first Seminole wars).

114.	1817 –The largest free African American church was formed. This was the African Methodist Episcopal Church in Charleston, South Carolina. It was one of the only Black Churches closed by the government for starting rebellions. It mixed Africanisms and Maat (reciprocity, reparations, etc.) with Christianity.

115.	1820 – A Sea Islands' planter owned the last ship that carried "slave cargo" to America. The ship was called the "Wanderer."

116.	1820 – First anti-slavery magazine was published in a Sea Island state. The magazine was called The Emancipator.

117.   1822 – "Gullah Jack" was Denmark Vesy's Commander of the Army. He was born in Angola, Africa which is an area where Gullah slaves were stolen. Denmark Vesy led the first recorded major revolt by the Gullahs. Africans attacked and fought Europeans (Swedish, Danes, Portuguese, Russians, etc.) that invaded Africa for slaves. Black people fought on slaves' ships, and attacked slave ships and constantly rebelled during slavery. They fought Europeans from all major religions (Christians, Jews, Moslems), as well as occult groups (Satin Worshipers). The slave women would feed white people ground up glass powder in their food. They would murder Caucasian enslavers and slave catchers. Two Black Slaves told Whites about a slave revolt plans. Because the Meritorious Manumission Act would grant them freedom for helping White people. They were found poisoned to death a few days after they told.

118.   1822 – Elijah McCoy invented the self-lubricating device that is used in cars, trains, planes, spaceships, and all type of machines. White People that wanted to know if an engine was self-lubricating would ask, "Is it the Real McCoy?" Elijah McCoy's mother was a Gullah lady.

119.   1822- South Carolina all White jury declared it was illegal for Blacks to wear fine cloth. The slaves must wear coarse cloth to remind them that they are inferior.

120.   1829- David Walker published "Walkers Appeal". He told slaves to become free they must kill their masters. "Anything a slave does to achieve freedom is honorable" quote of great

African American historian and teacher Dr. John Henry Clark.

121.   1830 – Largest indigo farms in America harvested by the Gullahs.

122.   1834 – Law passed that it is illegal to educate free Negroes and slaves. This was caused by Denmark Vesey and Nat Turner revolts. The Whites feared educated slaves would seek justice through any means. So-called "smart niggers" that could read and write were lynched. Many Blacks pretend to be stupid as a way to avoid being lynched or murdered. Currently, Smart Black children consider almost failing in school or being failed or going to jail as "Keeping it real". This is a symptom of Post Traumatic Slave Disorder.

123.   1842 – The USA declared war against slaves that included Gullahs. "The Negro War" was declared by General Jessup. He informed the War Department that runaway slaves were able and willing to try to defeat the USA.

124.   1843- Anna Madgigine Jai Kingsley an African Princess married her former Slave Master, after his death she spent her money to build cities for freed slaves.

125.   1850 –African American reservation. Gullahs and other slaves from "runaway slave" communities were chased by U.S soldiers across Texas into Mexico, where reservation existed for fugitives slaves.

126.   1850 – Texas Rangers were an official White mob that attacked and murdered Gullahs in

Texas. These Gullahs were being chased out of the Carolinas through Florida, New Orleans, through Texas, and eventually ran into Mexico. West African languages accents, Congo words, and African word order are noted in these states since that date.

127.   1852- Fredrick Douglas 4 July speech Rochester N.Y. said White Americans had "revolting barbarity and shameless hypocrisy., boast of liberty, greatness, equality, and are a bombast fraud, ... had a thin veil to cover up crimes which (genocide of Indians, enslavement of Blacks) would disgrace a nation of savages".

128.   1855 (circa) – "The Brick" Baptist Church built because Beaufort Baptist Church was integrated with 156 whites and 3,557 Blacks. The White Racist built a Brick Church so they could worship God properly (segregated, "Whites Only") because God did not want Whites worshipping with animals too human to be purely animals and too much animal to be purely human. They also believed that Whites and Blacks worshipping together would confuse God.

129.   1858 – First aid station/hospital. Aminta (Harriet Tubman) worked for the White Peoples Underground Railroad on Port Royal Island. Slave rebels, women, and children first created the slave escape hideouts and routes called the Underground Railroad. White businessmen politically sponsored their own version of the runaway railroad to weaken their southern business opponents. The White northern and southern slave owners would steal slaves of their White business competitor. They would use the stolen underground slaves to sell or get rid of

their competitor. The stolen so called free slaves decreased the profits of southern plantations causing default on bank loans that were made to northern bankers. The southern defaulted loans debt was then paid for by the government. And, the loss of southern plantations profits decreased money contributions to the confederates. Freeing the slaves was not their moral concern as they believed the slaves to have Drapetomania. Drapetomania is the mental illness that causes a slave to runaway. Harriet Tubman was involved in the underground railroad. She had Narcolepsy and would unpredictably fall asleep. She was hit in the head during slavery, and this caused the disease Narcolepsy. She led Colonel Montgomery and 300 Black Soldiers on an attack on the Confederate Army along the Combahe River S.C.

130.   1840- Trail of Tears March into Oklahoma Territory.   U.S Army at gunpoint forced Black Seminole Indians, Cherokee, Creek, and Choctaw Indians to leave the south and go to prison camps called Reservations.

131.   1859-1931 – During this time the slave livestock investments yielded the highest profit rate of return. The largest U.S. Wall Street stock investment was in the enslavement of the Africans. The U.S invested two billion dollars in the slavery business.   This was twice the amount spend on railroads.   Seventy percent of the USA foreign trade was from slave picked cotton.   The Wall Street stock market became wealthy from slave livestock in chain bondage (stocks and bonds). The most expensive and the most wanted cotton was Sea Islands cotton.   This cotton produced more revenue and sold for two to ten times the

price of regular cotton. Slave labor that picked cotton created the wealth that created U.S.A. Sugar cane slave plantations provided England, France, Germany, China, Indian, Arabs, and Portuguese with wealth.

132.   1859- "Dixie" Daniel Emmet a Black man from south moved up north and made the word Dixie popular. The treatment of Blacks in the north was very racist causing them to sing the words "I wish I was in Dixie (Southland)". No person seems to love or understand me all the blacks have bad luck stories to tell me. Blacks would sing the Bye, Bye Blackbird song lyric. "Bye, Bye Black birds (Southern birds). I will be coming home (to Dixie) late tonight".

133.   1860 –   Whites   segregated   their congregations by making the slaves (include Gullahs) sit in the so-called "Nigger Section." It was believed that whites and blacks praying together would confuse God.

134.   1860 – Twelve percent of Indian territory was occupied by the Gullahs and other African runaway slaves. The runaways had to be careful because Indian slave catchers would sell them back to White slave masters or sell them to Indians that had plantations that they operated for White people.

135.   1860 – The Sea Islands Secession Act. Edisto Island was the first confederate island to secede from the Union causing the Union Army to attack the Carolinas.

136.   1861 – Gullah and other slaves who escaped slavery in the South and moved to

Northern states and Canada were subjected to twice as much White Racism. They were treated badly by the racist Abolitionists who believed Negroes to be inferior. Many Northern states had slaves (i.e., Delaware, Rhode Island, Washington D.C, Ohio, Pennsylvania, New York, Maryland, Illinois, Massachusetts).

137.   1861 – The Civil War was called "Civil War Day" by White people and called by the Blacks "Gun Shoot Day". "Gun Shoot" is the Gullah name for the Union defeat of the Confederate Army. Whites abandoned the islands on this day, leaving the Blacks as the only inhabitants. The union Army did not free the slaves. The Emancipation Proclamation did not free slaves and allowed states to continue to have slaves. The Confederate Government and British emancipated slaves before Lincoln. The 13th Amendment was passed eight months after Abraham Lincoln's death. It ended chattel slavery. The 13th Amendment illegally made ex-slaves U.S. citizens and took away their Human Rights and gave them Civil Rights (Slave's Rights). Emancipated (means transfer of private ownership of slaves to government ownership of slaves). Slaves could be fined for so-called illegal behavior and be put back into slavery. If unable to pay the fine, they would have to work six months without pay for the state or a private business or a white citizen. This was worse than slavery.

John Jefferson, a Black Seminole (Indigenous
African American)
Enlisted in the 10th U.S Calvary

138.   1862- U.S Attorney General stated Black
people were not people of color, and therefore
they were ineligible to participate in the nation's
home steading, land grants or land rush
programs. This ended in 1902 when Blacks were
declared people of color. It was felt that Blacks
were too much like animals to be human and too
human to be animals.

139.   1862 – The Penn School started as an
educational experiment by Ellen Murry and Laura
Towne in Oaks Plantation. William Penn designed

the school for the domestication of the Gullahs. Despite his reputation as a fair and just "friend," Penn proved to be a bigot. He designed in the church separate sitting area pews for Blacks and whites. He stole land from Native Americans, and in Pennsylvania, he condemned a woman to death allegedly for being a witch.

140.   1862 – Black military organized during the Civil War. General Saxton was allowed to accept up to 5,000 Slaves as volunteer soldiers (this was similar to the military quotas still in use today). The Union Army was segregated the Blacks served as cooks, porters, servants to officers, worked in the laundry, clean living quarters, clean out house toilets, shine shoes, took care of horses etc.

141.   1862- Abraham Lincoln statements were; "My paramount objective in the (Civil War) struggle is to save the union, and is not to either save or destroy slavery", "Just as any other (white) man I am in favor of the superior position (White Supremacy) assigned to the White Race". In 1861 he stated "we didn't go into the war to put down slavery", and also stated "I am not in favor of bringing about in any way the social and political equality of the White and Black races". Lincoln had the war financed by loans from bankers (type of Wall Street). He essentially said "I have the confederate army to fight in front of me and the bankers in back of me. I am more afraid of the bankers". The bankers were considered ruthless thieves, that exploit people and to gain wealth, they are "gangsters" that are called "Banksters"

142.   1862 – Harriet Tubman's basket name (African) was Aminta. She baked goods for the Confederates in a house on Port Republic and Charles Streets in Beufort, S.C. Harriet Tubman was a functional title given to many women who helped free slaves. Harriet would say "Don't ever stop, keep going. If you want a taste of freedom keep going". Many slaves did not trust or believe her talks about being a free person. They threaten to tell the Slave Masters. To stop the Black Uncle Toms from telling the Slave Master, Harriet had to shoot them. It is believed that she killed with her rifle more Blacks than Whites.

143.   1863 – First strike by U.S. Army soldiers. Gullah and other Black soldiers refused to accept pay until they were paid the same rate as White Union Soldiers. The strike lasted 18 months. Blacks were paid $7.00 a month while White soldiers were paid $13.00. The Blacks were given an agreement to a raise or back pay after the War was over. They never honored the agreement of back wages. Anything agreement the White people legally write before you sign a White agreement check with the American Indians about White people's truthfulness. White people speak with a fork tongue (mix lies with the truth).

144.   1863 – Congressional Medal of Honor winners. Three Gullahs, who were erroneously called "Seminole Negro Indian Scouts," won the medals of honor.

145.   1863 – Gullah U.S. military regiment freed Black slaves. On June 3, 1863, Harriet Tubman and 250 armed Black soldiers of the 2nd Regiment led 727 slaves to freedom.

146.   1864 – Freedman's Banks, for Sea Islands' Gullahs was established by General Rufus Saxon. Gullahs deposited more than $240,000 and were swindled out of their savings by the U.S. Government and Saxon. Black ex-slaves money was given away to reimburse Slave Masters that loss money because their slaves were set free, help ex-confederate soldiers and newly arrived white immigrants.

147.   1864 – United States Colored Troops deposited $55,000 in the Freedman's Savings Bank of Beaufort. Black people used the money to purchase overpriced Sea Islands property. The sea Island property was given to Whites then they sold it to Black people. Aside from this, the government had already reimbursed them for the land loss with Black peoples money.

148.   1864 – U.S. Government gave Sea Islands to Gullahs. General William T. Sherman issued a Military Field Order Number 15, which designated that the Sea Islands and 30 miles inland from Charleston, South Carolina, be given to the Gullahs. It was not declared by U.S congress so President Johnson dismissed the order four months later. The only land the Gullahs received was land donated by the former Slave Masters. The former Slave Masters were reimbursed for their loss land with money stolen from saving accounts of Blacks in Freedman's Bank and the money the government accumulated from slavery investments.

149.   1865- The May 1st Memorial Day in Charleston, S.C. there were 257 dead from exposure and disease in a mass grave. They were re-buried by former slaves. They had a parade of

10,000 people which included 3,000 Black Children. While marching the dead bodies to a new grave they sang John Brown's Body. The event was then called Decoration Day.

150.   1865 –African American Secretary of State and State Treasurer, Francis L. Cardozo.

151.   1865 –African American Lieutenant Governor of South Carolina was Alonzo J. Ransier.

152.   1877 –Fire departments for a city with all African Americans. Gullahs formed fire companies, the Vigilant and Enterprise Company.

153.   1867 – The first African American school board for a major public school system was on Port Royal Island (Commonly referred to as Beaufort, South Carolina). The former slaves pattern it after The African Council of the Elders/Wise. Being an Elder/Wise is a function. Therefore, a 30-year-old adult could be classified as an Elder. Former slaves used the African educational structure to start the first public schools in the Carolinas.

154.   1867 – Beaufort County School Board was composed exclusively of African Americans: I.J. Cohen, Richard H. Gleaves, R.F. Bythewood, Walter Fuller, Landon S. Langley, Isaac Simmons, J.C. Rivers, Prince Rivers, Robert Smalls, Arthur Waddell, George Waddell, William Whipper, and Jonathan Wright.

155.   1859-68 –Deep sea divers in America. Gullah divers dived for phosphorous matter from an underwater fossil river 10 to 30 miles from the Wando River, south to the South Carolina's Broad

River. This phosphate was used as a fertilizer for plantation crops.

156.   1861-70 – Black U.S. Army troops used to put whites under martial law in Southern States in America. The Black Militia of 70,000 was the largest group of armed ex-slaves in America. This made defeated Confederate states very angry and many Black Soldiers were lynched in their uniform.

157.   1861-70 – Most influential newspaper in the African American communities of the South. The Missionary Record, was published in South Carolina by Richard H. "Daddy" Cain.

158.   1861-70 – "The Gullah Statesman," Robert Smalls held state office for six years and served five terms in the U.S. Congress. During the Civil War this former slave and his crew of men, women, and children captured a confederate steamer (The Planter) and gave it to the Union Army during the Civil War. A bust of Mr. Smalls is at the Tabernacle Baptist Church in Beaufort, South Carolina.

159.   1861-70 – Senator John C. Calhoun issued a warning that South Carolina would become Africanized. Added to this, African King Menelik gave several million dollars in gold to the United States to be given to ex-slaves. Senator Thaddeus Stevens made the reparational promise which was never a U.S.A congress approved law to give each Negro "40 acres and a mule," which is currently equal to more than $500,000. The US Government stole king Menelik's gold and put it in Fort Knox and has never given the gold or profit from interest to Black people.

160.   1861-70 – Largest cotton press in the world was in Port Royal.

161.   1861-70 – One of the first Black historians was a Sea Islands resident named Martin R. Delaney. He was an African explorer, an agent for the Freedman's Bureau and historian.

162.   1861-70 – Railroad coaches manufactured on Port Royal Island South Carolina with Gullah slave laborers. The Black people made coaches that Black Pullman Porters work on. The Pullman Palace Car Company had Black railroad workers that went on strike in 1894. President Grover Cleveland sent troops to stop the Black Strikers, 15 were killed, and 60 were injured. The striker's wages were cut in half and most were fired.

163.   1861- Southern Confederate Soldiers and Union Soldiers took their Black slaves with then into combat.

164.   1863- General Lee, reported that the main method of getting information from our enemy's plan is through negro's communication network of quilts, wash tub drums, and songs.

165.   1874 – Father Divine (1874-1965) was born on the Gullah Sea Island of Hutchinson Island, Georgia. He was a famous religious leader who used strict moral and social rules as part of his teachings (no smoking, drinking, or cosmetics).

166.   1881 – Dr. York W. Bailey, first Gullah medical doctor. Bailey was born on St. Helena

Island. He used herbs and traditional medicine and drugs to help his patients. Bailey used the African barter system and accepted chickens and foods as payments.

167.   1883 – Shoemaking machine invented by African American Jan E. Matzelinger. His mother was from West Africa (Rice Coast Gullahs).

168.   1887 – Marcus Garvey (1887-1940) created an international economic and social movement. He was born on the Gullah island of Jamaica; where Gullah people were tortured until they accepted slavery or murdered, or raped if they refused to be slave. His slogans were "Africa for Africans," and "One God, One Aim, One Destiny." He started the use of the colors red, black, and green on the African American flag.

169.   1887 – V. H. James was born in Carolinas. He organized at Howard University the first art gallery that was controlled and directed by African Americans.

170.   1880- Black Commander Richard Etheridge taught Black people to read and write and pass Civil Service Examination. His family was from the Gullah areas.

171.   1889 –Africans in America (Gullah Ex-Slaves) had four units that fought in the Spanish-American war. Some soldiers that rode with Teddy Roosevelt's "Rough Riders" were given a dishonorable discharge on a claim that they raped a white woman. In 1980, it was changed to an honorable discharge.

172.   1891 –African Ex-slaves demanded reparations (back wages). Gullah Congressman, Thomas E. Miller, asked that plantation checks issued to Gullahs by whites be honored by the state.   Their checks were not honored and became worthless

173.   1900 – Gullah music made popular in America. George Gershwin copied Gullah music and composed the musical, Porky and Bess about a drug addicted female prostitute, which was used to degrade and inferiorized the Black race. He studied the Gullah music in Charleston and traveled to the Islands to steal the authentic sounds, rhythms, and copyright them.   Stolen Black people's music by the Gershwin brothers and many other White musicians continuously get paid royalty money for slaves and Black Americans tunes and songs with White people's lyrics re-phrased from black lyrics.

174.   1900 – The song, Michael Row De Boat Ashore, was copied my missionaries from the Gullah boatmen that sang the song it as they worked on the ferry boats in downtown Beaufort (Carteret and Bay Streets).

175.   1920 – Gullah race riot was on May 2, 1910, Black people attacked wounded, and killed one United States Army soldier at Fort Freemont, off Land's End Road on St. Helena Island. The United States Government failed to prosecute or jail any Blacks involved. The White newspaper failed to explain the incident beyond it being a social evening that erupted in violence.

176.   1926 – First cotton fabric used to pave a road. The Cotton Road was in Chapin County, South Carolina.

177.   1932 – The George Washington quarter (25 cents) had a picture of an eagle on one side. George Washington owned, raped, and murdered slaves. Martha Washington owned 153 slaves, she whipped them, cut off women's breast, pulled off fingers, cut up and disfigured women's faces that had sex with George and caused slave women to have miscarriages by throwing them down steps if she suspected they were pregnant by George. Martha upon her death freed the slaves. George made his fortune off slavery, was the largest alcohol businessmen in America, and had marijuana plantations.

178.   1900- Henry William De Saussure (owner of the Gold Eagle Hotel on New Street near Bay Street) designed the American Eagle used on USA money. It is the Black African symbol of Isis and Maat (justice, peace, balance, harmony, propriety, etc.).

Slave Revolt Affirmation

During slavery/colonialism, the Black people on the Continent and Diaspora (i.e., Gullah) would secretly meet in the bush or cabins to tell African folktales and/or perform Maatian (Theme of justice, harmony, balance, reciprocity, etc.) rituals and ceremonies. They would organize military counterattacks (rebellions) against the Europeans. Many chants of encouragement and positive affirmations were recited in order to keep the spirit of freedom, culture and military consciousness alive. The militant slave men, women, and children understood that without a military to protect them and attack their White enslaving enemies, freedom cannot and will not exist. The following are a few examples of affirmations:

Du Free-dum	Freedom is ours
E knot de tongue	I promise
Du Free-dum	Freedom is ours
Fuhr ride de buckra frame	To fight the Whites
Uh tek back de tief um	And, take back all that they stole from us
Du Free-dum	Freedom is ours
Ef e no do um Gawd tek e soul	If I don't may I die = God take my soul
Du Free-dum. Fuhr tru. Du Free-dum.	Freedom is ours. It is true. Freedom is ours.

Swahili	English
Eh! Eh! Bomba! Heu! Heu!	We swear to defeat (destroy)
Canga, bafia te Canga. moune de le	The Whites and all they possess
Conga, do ki la	Let us die rather than
Congo, li	Fail to keep this vow

How to Speak Conversational Gullah

The Gullah conversational language, like all African languages is organic (living). Gullah is alive, constantly changing and can be improvised upon. It is a spontaneous improvised rap language. In speaking Gullah, you should mix and match sentences and words from these conversations in order to communicate. The purpose of language is to communicate, not to be grammatically correct. Language reflects the current and past history of a people. The sounds and rhythms of the words will lead you to good combinations. The more you speak it, the better. These are just a few Gullah sentences and words that you can use to get started on your cultural journey.

Conbensate	Conversation
Yello	**Hello**
Whu do um? Or Wuh Fuhr do?	How are you?
Wuh ya name?	**What is your name?**
Me name yiz.....	My name is ......
Who e yiz?	**Who are you?**
Me name yiz........	My name is........
Glad fuh saa'b yah	**I am glad to meet you.**
E too glan fuh see yah	I am glad to see/meet you also
Yuh duh talk em Gullah?	**Can you speak Gullah?**
Uh ent nebbuh crack me teet Fuhr Gullah much	I cannot speak much Gullah.
Wat ya gwi do?	**What are you going to do?**
Wuh e wan?	What do you want to do?
Lea fuh fess-tibble, kar, Hoe-tell	**Go directly to the festival, car, hotel**
Ya fuh gone?	Are you going?
Uh gwine tuhmorroh, Day clean.	**I am going tomorrow, today**

Gullah	English
E uh fine day	It is a nice day.
E yiz fuh tru	Yes, it is.
Un tie e mont	**Let's talk.**
Uh binnah talk	I've been talking.
Uh mos dead wid de loansum	**I've been by myself**
Wuh ya duh talk bout?	What do you want to talk about?
Yeddy me?	**Did you hear me?**
Uh nebbuh yeddy	I did not hear you.
Uh yent sub uh kin fin num kar, hoe-tell, etc.	I cannot find the, car, hotel etc.
E obuh yanduh	**It s/he is over there**
Tengk ya	**Thank you**
Berry Welden	You are very welcome.
Gib de time uh day?	What time is it?
Cal um seben de clock	It was seven o'clock
Wuh de time be done bruk-up?	**What time is it over?**
Uh lee	Early.
Nuf people bunch-up innar	**There are many people there.**
Cu leh wez gqine	**Come, let's go.**
Uh gwine set een de cheer	I am going to sit in this chair
Uh waa'k til uh agonize me bone	I walked until I am exhaust
E onduhstan	**I(s/he) understand**
E hab plaz ene haa't	I have a place in my heart for you.
Bimeby un gwine de Fess-tibble, hotel, etc.	After awhile, I am going to the festival, hotel, etc.
E a mout dry up	**You, I, s/he stopped talking.**
Uh gwine lick back en kin crack ya teet	I will come back and Yah talk

Useful Sentences

E gone bedout e mek e mannus — S/he left without saying goodbye.

Uh yeh hab Cajun fuh meet um — I am glad to meet you.

E posit e wud — S/he didn't say a word

De compuh say longum — S/he talks a long time

E mek de long tark — S/he gossips

E bex long e mout — S/he used cursing

Dat beat me time — I can't believe it

It ah sickenin ting — It is worrisome

E paw tun puss'n — S/he is an important person

Den cun fuh shum — They come to see her/him

Uh spon d uh yent know un — They act like they don't know me, us, you.

E cheap um yah — S/he insulted you

E ain't hab all de buttons — S/he does not have a good sense.

Pay um no min — Ignore them, her, him, it.

E bow dashus — S/he is bold.

E projic wid um — S/he interferes.

E dribuh fus news — You drive next.

Yah dribuh duh two time. — You drive twice.

Wuh de mout box up? — Why are you frowning?

Oonuh suck e teet. — You disagree

Lee ax um — I asked.

Yah no fuhr always eet Out de same spoon. — We don't always agree.

Uh gwine tuhreckly. — I am leaving soon.

E dunk yua. — I don't care.

Wich pussun b'long un? — Which person does this belong to?

E gon spang. — Go quickly

Shut de do e car, room, etc. — Close the car, room, door etc.

Tengky fuhr eberything e cum lick back.
Thanks for everything. I will come back.

Me gwine.
I am going

Wen fuhr las time e fuhr see yah?
When was the last time I saw you?

E no fuhr memba.
I don't remember

Cudda layed yee onna yah enna
It could have been

Augus, Septemba, Actowba:
August, September, or October.

E tangled lee haad.
I am confused.

Ub benna swim longso e noh swim moe.
I swam so long I could not swim any more.

Oonuh tek dem pic-char?
You take our picture?

Wuh de camarah.
Hold the camera.

Move yah haad/esef dat way.
Move your head/yourself that way.

Tap yah su.
Stop there.

Mek teet show ye tuh yez
Smile

Mek wen yah reddee.
Tell me when you are ready.

Uh ben spen me time onnah beech.
I spend all my time at the beach.

Uuh tote le towil wid yuh?
Did you take a towel with you?

Going Out to Eat

Dey don git bittle/food.	Let's go and eat.
E belly pinch um.	S/he is hungry.
Gi we som bittle.	Give me some food
Ennybody gwine wid me?	Anybody going with me.
Yuh fuhr gwine?	Are you going?
Uh hab moanee fuh bittle/food?	I have money for food.
Uh done fuh eeting de day.	I have already eaten.
Uh hab nut eet.	I have not eaten.
Dey ent hab nutt n fuh eet.	I/we did not have anything to eat.
E brakfus eet?	Did you eat breakfast?
Un ben reddee fuh brakfus, dinnah, etc.	I am ready for breakfast, dinner, etc.
Fallow me tudda ress-runt	Follow me to the restaurant
E kant wait.	I cannot wait.
Lukkuh dat pussu pack up de mout.	Look at that person stuff themselves.
E wah nuff bittle.	I want plenty to eat.
Dese caffe bun pon e mout lips.	The coffee burns my lips.
Yuh bittle/foo nayam betta ter fuhr. ussum	Your food tastes better than ours.
Gi e ah lilli moe bittle.	Give me more to eat.
E blang time wate ponde bittle.	I have waited a long time for food.
Wuh dem people de nyam?	What are those people eating?
De chillun/chile n yam.	The children/child have/has eaten.
Uh know wuffuh done eet.	I don't know what eat.
Uh studee head.	You think about it.
Wuh e wan eet?	What do you want to eat?
Oonuh hab swit toot	You like sweets?
E wan tas'e' mout bittle/foot.	I want something good to eat.

E gwine tuh gedduh fuhr de ress-runt.	Let's go to the restaurant.
Wuffuh ress-runt kin chuss wuh yah?	Which restaurant should we choose?
No, uh yent fuh go de ress-runt.	I do not know which restaurant to go to.
Ef e gwine pay fuhr um?	Are you going to pay?
Uh anduddah wu'se done pay. fuh tru.	I will pay another day. That's the truth.
Dem gwine fuh bye bittle. Cum leh we gon.	S/he is going to buy food Let's go.
Uh gwine set een eeet.	I am going to sit and eat.
Bress de bittle.	Bless the food.
Tek e pledjuh de bittle	Enjoy your food.
Pledjuh e sefe	Enjoy our self.
Uh eet mawn.	I want to eat more.
Bittle wen et lib fuhr.	Food is all you live for.
Id tas lik sum moe.	It tastes good.
Fuh satify fuhr trute.	I am satisfied.
E tummach bittle fuh eat.	S/he ate too much.
Enybody wuh tote de bittle tuh dem?	Anybody want to take food to the others?
Dem gwine fuh bye bittle. How lawn e stan so?	They, s/he will buy food. How long have we been here?
E yent figguh fuh go.	I don't know.
E mek ansuh suh e yent d-um.	I do not know the answer.
Come leh we gwine.	Let's go

Travel

Mek fuh?	Go!
Co'se uh gwine.	Of course, I am going.
Wuh long mout um?	Why are you pouting?
Le'm	Let them, her, him, etc.
E one ob we people.	S/he is one of us.
We se'f gwin.	We will go with you. Or We went ourselves.
E swit mout fren.	S/he is a good friend.
Mek mount um yez tuh yez	Smile
Lick bak gwine wid yah de kar, hoe-tell, fess-tibble.	We will go back with you to the car, hotel, festival, etc.
E look lukkuh anuddah puss'un	S/he, it looks like someone else.
Ya fictive?	Are you kinfolk/related?
E bu out wid de laugh.	S/he laughed.
E full up nice un up.	S/he is full of flattering talk.
Wuh ya knot ya face?	Why are you frowning?
Cu leh we gwine.	Come, let's go.
Yah gwine bidout um	You go without me.
Yah cyan leenfuh um.	You can leave without me, them, etc.
Uh waa gone de hoe-tell, kar, fess-tible, etc.	I want to go to the hotel, car,
How dem kin lik back de hoe-tell, kar, etc.	How can I get back to the hotel, car, etc.
E need fuh gon back tuh de...	I need to go back to the....
Lick back gwine.	Turn around and go.
E gwine pon de tour.	I am going on the tour.
Oonuh hab in-gin sic.	You have engine problems?
E affen rent ah kar.	I want to rent a car.
Ho mucha mile fra yah be gwine?	How many miles to go?

E yent gwine de, kar, hoetel etc.	I am going to, car, hotel, etc.
Uh gwine	I am going
Uh yeddy um.	I am ready
Uh yen k no w'eddub don gwine?	I don't know whether they are going.
Yah dribuh de kar	You drive the car.
Yah dribuh fus gwine	You drive first.

Chillum Talk / Children Talk

Mek so de chillum/ chile gone?	Where are/is the children/child?
Uh yent shum.	I did not see them.
De chillum/chile gone.	The children have left.
Gone at fuhr um.	Go after them.
Uh shum.	I see them.
De chillum/chile gone fuh shum gen.	The children/child are/is gone again.
Dem beat du't tun.	They ran as fast as s/he could.
Weh e iz?	Where is/are s/he, they?
E yent dey.	S/he, they were/was not there.
Light out fuhr um.	Go after them.

Parent/Child Conversation

Weh e be gwine?	Where were you?
Ub bin saach fuhr.	I have been looking for you.
Wuh e do?	What have you been doing?
De wadde plash all obub um.	The water splashed all over me.
Bex, long e ye ye.	I was so angry I cried.
Nebbuh hapee no mo.	I was unhappy.

Ef id ben wusser, ah be most dead.
If it was worse, I would have(drown) died.

E cum fuh see yah cus e tangledy.
I came to see you because I was confused.

Uh yent shum yah.
I did not see you.

Ah went fuhr play til dry.
So, I went to play until I got dry.

De boduhr um tummuch.
It bothered me so much.

Yah no wiffud me do?
You know what I'll do?

Ah no ya befo e bawn. Fuhr trute. Naw wha tek ya long so.
I know you well. Now, tell me what took you so long.

E choir fuh liss'ne.
I will be quiet and listen.

Children Words / Chillum Wuds

The children/child are/is very obedient.
Dem chillum/chile berry bejun

The children/child behave badly.
Dem chillum/chile behave too bad.

The child lost its parents.
De chile los e parents.

The children/child are/is
Dem chillum/chile too stiff.

That child is a good dancer.
De chile know wud how fuhr drop legs.

They danced a long time.
De da-ance tillum feet batam burn.

When I left they cried.
Weh e dey left dem cry.

The children love to play sing, dance, etc.
Nyung chillum lub fuhr play, sing, dance, etc.

Get away from there.
Git way fum ya.

Gather in the park
Gedduh tuh de paa'k

There was an accident
Uh ack sident bin hab.

Here I am.
Yuh un es.

Boy
Man chile

Girl
Ooman chile.

Child that wets on themselves is childish, or immature person.
Piss tail chile.

Shopping

Wuh cum fuh see?	What are you looking for?
Wuh e wan?	What do you want?
Unrabble de mout.	Talk about it.
E cum fuh see closes.	I want to see clothes.
Pick wuh ya chose.	Select what you want.
Wuh dat iz?	What is it?
Wuh ya duh shop fuh?	What are you shopping for?
Ub bin saa ch uh fuhr.	I have been looking for . . .
E uh berry soon ooman, man, pussun.	I am a stylish(classy) woman, man, person.
E tukkah.	It is similar.
Uh no fuh do um.	Don't do it (buy it).
E sane lukkuh.	It looks the same.
Trau c ye ye.	Look closely.
E de cyan spek fry yen wu't.	It looks worthless.
Uh bye um fum yanduh.	Buy another place.
Dat cos tummach.	It costs too much.
W'en ya com de fuhr deal, e mus no fuhr deal.	When you look for a bargain you must know a bargain.
E canc um.	Take a risk. Risk it.
Luk onduh neet dat.	Look underneath that.
Wuh e suh?	What did you see?
Yah tangled.	I am confused.
Hep um wid dese.	Help me with this.
E suh de cost?	What is the price?
Wuh e wort?	What is it worth?
Do um.	Do it. Buy it.
Uh sho ent wan lef til bye um.	I am not going until I buy it.
Yah tiefin de ting.	You are getting it at a steal. Or It is a cheap price.
Fuh worree nun.	Don't worry.
E suck e teet.	I disagree

Us spen all de dolluh tuh de sto, fess-tibble, etc.	We spent all my money at the store, festival, etc.
E gwine fuhr bye de ting?	Are you going to buy the thing?
Shop, been weh e lib fuhr.	Shopping is what I live for.
Ah wan fuhr pay.	I want to pay for it.
Uh en fuh credik cha'age um. fuhr change.	I want to charge it on my credit card.
Oonuh pleez, kin gimme	May I have change.
E bye tummach tings.	You buy too many things.
Un mus min e bidness.	You mind your own business.
Yah gun bye towing jisso.	You buy for no particular reason.
E haa'dly kin spen.	You hardly can pay for it.
E bin dry lon so e spen.	It's been a long time since I have spent
Cyan no tel yah enne ting.	I cannot tell you anything money..
Ef e bi dis oonuh no kan bi dat.	If you buy this, you cannot buy that.
E mek leh walk roun little fus.	Let me walk around a little first.
De cos yiz bettar obah dese.	The price is better over there.
Mek leh try obad de plaz, sto, etc.	Let's try over there at that place, store, etc.
E nuh wan des sum.	I don't want it.
Tekkah lee dollah offah e buy um.	Take off a dollar and I will buy it.
Wea de price drap e lick back.	When the price drops, I will return.

Wedduh	Weather
Dat rain uh day clean.	It is raining today.
Yass, e dun rain haad. fuhr trute.	Yes, it is really raining hard.
E duh wedduh	Is it storming.
Yuh fuhr gwine?	Are you going?
Pen pun on de wedduh.	It depends on the weather.
E too daa'k fuhr dem go.	It's too dark to go.
Dem cand'l lite n.	It's night time.
E	It is ....
....nigh um	....night
....fuss-daa'k	....evening
....so-lean	....sundown
E uh fine day.	It is a nice day.
Tuhmorruh uh fine day.	Tomorrow will be a nice day.
E uh-ly	It is early.

Health

E yent hel tee.	I am healthy.
E yent sic.	I am sick.
De flam graff e haad.	I have a head cold.
De col e hab um.	I have a cold.
E he'th stan po.	You look sick.
Dey bin sick	They are sick.
E sugah gut me.	I have diabetes.
Uh gwine all do uh fill sowtuh so.	I am going although I don't feel like it.
De misery bin hab um	I don't feel well
Yah aggabate tummach.	You worry too much.
De ritis agonize me bone.	I have arthritis
E nature gwine.	I have a sex problem, impotence, frigidity.
Me teet hab hurten een agga-bate.	I have a tooth ache.

Ub ben feel likkah yiz gonna drap sic.	I feel like I am getting sick.
E hab lee blood presha.	I have high blood pressure.
Don't press me nerves.	Don't stress me.
Oonuh helf cud-dah betta do-um.	Your health could be better.
Yuh haben fus aid kit?	Do you have a first aid kit?
Le horse-biddle tek pleez.	Take me to the hospital.

Useful Words

As'm	hands
Adduh'res	others
Dekase	because
Bex tek um	angry
Buckra	white person
Cum Fuh	come
Crab crack	eat crabs
Dig dut	ran
De bey graff	grab
Ent	is/are/does/did
Else so	otherwise
En	and
En ting	other things
E stan	It is so
E	he, she, it
Fr'en	friend
Fus	first
Flam	phlegm, mucus, cold, sinus
Greese e mout	taste good
Gree	agree
Lee	the
Low	admit
Light out	go after
Likeso	also

Min um	take care of it, him
Nyam	to eat
Oonuh	you
Ooman	woman
Paa'k	park
Papuh	paper
Peruse	slowly
Pun top	on top
Pit	put
Pussun	person
Rid e frame	fight
Ramify raw n	rude, unmannerly
Sugar num	without
Tief	steal
Ye Ye	eye

Gullah Proverbs

A pound of mouth shut, worth ounce explainin'.

Promisin talk don cook rice.

Det wan ditch you arn fuh jump.
Death is one ditch you have to jump.

Ebery day ya tote lee buckit tuh de well in disa dey
de bottam he gwine drop outta.
Every day one takes chances, but one
day your luck will run out.

Emptea sack can't stand upright alone.

Ef you hol you mad e would kil e by glad.
If you hold your anger it will kill
all your happiness.

Er goo run bettuh dan uh bad stan.
An Alternate tactic is better that failing with an old tactic.

E by bac is fit to de bu'den.
Every person is able to carry his own burden.

Hart don't mean every ting mough say.
Sin is ezee to stan dan shaim.

Sad we got to be burnt fore we learn.

Still watar gits stale an scummy too kwit.
It can waash de way sin.
Don't wait too long to apologize because it will be
stale, but it still is an apology.
Tit fuh tat, but tar fuh fat, et yuh.
Kilt my dawg, I kilt yuh cat.
For every action, there is an equal reaction.

Trouboil goin fall! Ain't goin fall on da ground!
Goin fall onna sum boddee.

Mo rain, mo ress, but fair wedder bin bess.
Onpossible (impossible) ta git straight
wud from crook kit timber.

Mos hook fish don't hep dry hominy.
An almost hooked fish does not improve
the taste of hominy grits.

Tongue and teth don't always git along.

De Watermelon Gullah Language Story

In 1840, a runaway slave from Wallace Plantation was caught steeling watermelon on Fripp Plantation.

Some massa an some oberseer bery cruel. One nite, a man go in de feel to git wader mellon. He be bery hungry for dey ain gib de slaves nuff to eat annee time. De guard catch him.

Shut him up all dat day, wait fo hi tide. Tide jes as hi as tis now.

Den, he tak fo mens an dey duck him, an duck duck himan duck him twell he mos dead. Den dey lay him big log, an dey two mens hol arms up an tother mens hol he legs an deoberseer beet him til bled jes gush. An de womans an demans an de chitlin all holler. "Yo gwine kell him." I knowed I ben stanin rite yere jes as it ben ye'tiddy. Den dey pit him in cart an him drive to de main road an dey den com to de certon spot. Dey trow him out like a bag manure an he lie rite dere an day clean he be dead.

De oberseer bin rested an pit in de jail an dey gwing hung him, but de massa pay him out an let him go. Neber let him be comin back here dough.

Slave Woman

Crops Harvested by the Gullahs

1520 Figs, olives, oranges, peaches, apricots,
grapes
1600 Pine, pitch turpentine, silk
1680 Rice
1750 Indigo
1790 Cotton
1830 Phosphate
1920 Free Gullahs: tomatoes, lettuce, cabbage,
radish

Unsuccessful Crops: Ginger

Gullah Technology

Ham is a European Biblical word for Khem (Black), just as Nubia, Sudan, Moors, and Ethiopian are their words for Black Africans. The Kemetic Africans, dating back to 1.7 million BCE [Before Common Era] came from Southern Africa from an area commonly called Sudan. They traveled to Egypt (KMT) before 5,000 BCE A drought around the Sahara Desert area in 2,500 BCE caused some Africans to move to Europe, India, China, Japan, and the Middle East. Ancient Africans brought the concept of one God and knowledge (Karate, Acupuncture) and basically civilized the colored and white races. Despite this, the Europeans (whites) remain a predatory race that prey upon others' human and natural resources (land, gold, water, metal, food, crops) and human resources (slaves, wage slaves). Predators attack the weak as well as strong because they are hungry for food and/or natural and human resources.

African people taught Africa's greatest gift to the world, "Human Relationship." The East Kemetic languages are spoken by the ethnic groups of Somalia, Masai, and Galla. The Galla (Gullah) moved to Africa's west coast. Galla were free Africans put into slavery by the East Indians, Chinese, Asians, Greeks, Romans, Arabs and then the Europeans. African people were not allowed to speak or write in African language, dress in African clothes, use African jewelry, educational systems, medicine, artifacts, customs, ceremonies, rituals, or treat women divinely. They could not use African moral values or their Kemetic spirituality (called Pagan Religion by Euro-Christians, Euro-Moslems, Euro-Jews) or practice "Maat" (truth, righteousness, and justice). Galla (Gullah) people brought their knowledge of "Human Relationship" and technology to America.

Dating back to 10,000 BCE and pre-Egypt, the documented ancient African skills and knowledge brought to America and the European world were many. They included engineering, agriculture, irrigation, the invention of the wheel, the zodiac, the fire sticks (matches), the process of boiling water, astronomy, navigation, mills, cultivation, the theater, construction, wheel barrow, metal (tin) work, carpentry, philosophy, music, cereals, the sail ships, pulleys, levers, massage, metric system, government, law, pants, medicine, physics, calculus, sewing, architecture, business, textile industry, bowling, tic-tac-toe, money, chemistry, herbology, plumbing, dance therapy, gymnastics, language pendulums, bureaucracy, kingmanship, chess, priesthood, religions, cosmetology, swings, the toilet, soap, fans, magnets, preservation of nature (ecology), fairy tales (rites of passage), writing, natural birth, pharmacology, farming tools, dentistry, ophthalmology, hot (green) house, the concept of the number zero, steam bath, clock, civilization, etc.

Gullah people were given names based upon African ethnic groups that they came from, such as the Krio (called Creole) and the Kissi people (called Geechee).

Gullah Hag Stories

Gullah "Hag" stories reflect African folk beliefs, and are firmly rooted in mythology and relate to wisdom, justice, Maat, and spirituality. In African Mythology a "Hag" is a spirit that visits the living in order to transport information or messages from the spirit world or those that are dead. "Hags" are similar to an aura (electromagnetic cloud) and can be felt or in some way sensed to be present around the living. There are "Bo-Hags." The African word "Bo" means far away, so a "Bo-Hags." is a spirit (ancestral) from far away, Africa, or a deceased relative. Hag stories may seem like mumble jumble or superstitions from slavery days. However, these stories carry keys to wisdom and are not as fragmented or irrelevant as they sound.

In ancient Africa, (includes Egypt), the aura was respected and acknowledged to be a living part of life. Gullah "Hag" stories reflect African culture and acknowledge that the aura (could be of deceased ancestors) is a living part of life. In fact, the aura, (called KA by Egyptians) is made primarily by the Pineal gland. The pineal gland makes a liquid called Melanin. The pineal gland is a pea-size gland in the center of the brain. Melanin makes an aura and melanin elements continuously vibrate during life and after a person's death. Melanin carries genetic information, influences all bodily activities, emotions, actions, thinking, growth, extrasensory perception, nerve impulses, muscles, metabolism, and immunity, aside from giving African peoples' skin its black color (Power and Science of Melanin L. Afrika). In any case, the "Hag" stories and legends have a vague connection to ancient African scientific information. The stories demonstrate how African science fragmentally survived through an enslavement, which outlawed and castrated African culture, science, and spirituality. The Hag stories are a testimonial to the Black peoples stubbornness to retain as much of African culture and mythology as possible and live as a spiritual people. Black people (Gullahs) are spiritual people and they are able to feel or sense the presence of an aura. Black people have many stories for activities, misbehaviors, adventures, and conversations with spirits or auras, commonly called "Hags."

In Egyptian Mythology, the first written Hag-type stories appear. For example, one such Hag story is about the Goddess Nut (Pronounced Noot). Goddess Nut wanted to find out the secret power of Ra (Sun God). In the story, Ra represents the sun or the attribute of God to make living energy. Nut was the attribute of God to create. Goddess Nut created the sky or heaven. Ra became very old and always took long walks in order to look at his creations of the water, wind, plants, animals, and the earth. On one of his walks he accidentally stepped on a dart, Goddess Nut poisoned Ra with a dart, causing him to go into a deadly deep sleep. She told Ra she could save him from death if he gave her his secret powers. Ra eventually whispered the secret word of power into Nut's ear and she saved him from death. Nut, who was symbolically a Hag wanted to get power. She used sleep or the time when the soul leaves the body to travel to get Ra to release the power words. In this story, Ra and Nut represent the two great truths that each person must know. These truths were taught during the holistic classes called the "Rites of Passage". The bipolar truths are commonly known as Good/Evil, Right/Wrong, Man/Woman, Birth/Death, Night/Day, Body/Spirit, etc. If a person is not following his spiritual purpose in a Godly life, then the Hag can disturb him, upset him, or take him in a deadly sleep. It was believed that the Hag (also called Hap, Hapi, etc.) was coming to transport the soul back to Africa, but the soul could not go unless it got rid of the Baraka (White Man's behavior, culture or the ordeal).

The Hag story is reflected in the name for the George Gershwin stolen Gullah musical titled, "Porgy and Bess". In Egyptian mythology, when Ra became an old man, he was given the name Bess. Traditionally, African Kings or Priests were responsible for communicating between the people and God. In other words, all the King's decisions were supposed to be checked by the will of God first and the Maat legal system second. African Kings were given nicknames that symbolized communicating between God and Earth. A fish symbolized transporting people's wishes, actions, and ideas between man and God. King Menes, of the First Egyptian Dynasty, was given the nickname Catfish(Porgy). Incidentally, Mene's name translates to Memphis. Therefore, the city of Memphis, Tennessee is named after this African man. In any case, the fish, Porgy, is a symbol directly related to Africa. The two characters in the musical "Porgy and Bess", is indirectly related to African mythology in which the Hag's desires to transport (take) your spirit out of your body.

The origin of the word, Hag, can be found in the so-called Egyptian Book of the Dead, written 1500 BCE. The correct name for the book is The Book of Coming Forth by Day and by Night. Hag is an Africanized English word. Hag or Haxe or Hex stems from Hermes. Hermes means Thoth in the Egyptian language. Thoth is the spirit that reads the 42 affirmation of innocence. The Ten Commandments are derived from the African 42 declaration (affirmation) of innocents. These declarations of innocence had to be confirmed correctly before a person's soul could enter heaven. Consequently, Hags like to read commandments, proverbs, newspapers, or scriptures. Hags are still secretly looking for the more magic words of power in proverbs, newspapers, etc. Hags often sit down at a Hag stool (mushroom) to read. Gullahs would let mushrooms grow near their house so Hags could sit down and read instead of coming into the house.

Hags are believed to stop a restful sleep. While in a dream a Hag may hold your body in a frozen position while you try to move your body. Hags may stop you from hollering out loud for help while in the dream story of a horrible or dangerous nightmare. A Hag may disguise itself as a human being. Sometimes, it is believed that a Hag may possess a human body. Hags may take off the spirit skin and leave it outside your house before entering. There are tests to determine whether a person is a Hag. For example, sprinkle salt on the suspected Hag's shadow. If the person is a Hag, they will get nervous or shake or appear in pain. Sprinkle salt around the house and if a Hag takes off its skin, the salt will get inside the skin and irritate the Hag when they put the skin back on their invisible body. Sometimes, a "Bad News Fly" or "Shoo Fly" will buzz around your head to warn you that a Hag is coming to your house or is in the house with you. In African Mythology, Shoo or Shun is the spirit that helps you to climb up the ladder (Jacob's ladder) to enter heaven. The "Shoo Fly" is trying to lift your spirit up or help you to be aware that a Hag is present. Some Hags like to drink alcohol to enjoy parties. Hags may come to social gatherings and act silly or start trouble, argument, or a fight. You can lay a broom on the floor in the front doorway entrance to your house. This will stop a suspected hag from coming into your house. The broom can stop a Hag from leaving your house. If someone stays in your house eating up your food or have a very long conversation or spread gossip or lies, or seems to be wearing out their welcome to your house, they may be a Hag. It is best to put your broom behind the front door and then the suspected hag will leave. Sometimes a Hag will hide in your clean clothes that are left outside on the clothesline overnight. Some Hags are bald and will use hair left in a comb to cover the bald spots on their heads or put a spell or curse on the hair to make a person do something that the Hag cannot do in its ghost form. It is usually advised to take hair out of your comb and burn all hair left in your comb and brush so a Hag cannot take it for evil purposes. A few dogs or birds such as a crow can see Hags. It is believed that the crow's hollering sound is "Hag! Hag!" It is believed that when a person sneezes, their soul may leave their body. If the Hag does not take the sneezing persons soul, you traditionally say, "God Bless you." A safe way to protect the soul while sneezing is to say "Hag! Hag! Shoo!" This will stop a Hag from entering your body. It is good to carry a proverb or a favorite scripture in your pocket. Gullah slaves carried African words written on paper in Amulets and wore with protection words in it. Amulets around the neck. If a proverb, piece of newspaper, or scripture was not available, then they would wear a little bag with a plant called, Asafoetida. Asafoetida has a horrible smell and was called the Devil's Bowel Movement (dung). It has a smell that is similar to a rotten egg mixed with garlic and pig manure. Hags do not like the smell of Asafoetida and it is doubtful that you will like it.

Hag stories store traces of Gullah African heritage and fragments of the Maat wisdom needed to live a family-centered life and a God-centered life. The use of the broom in Hag remedies symbolizes God because brooms were used to sweep African religious temples and to sweep the village compound before the performance of rituals, and ceremonies and crown a new king or leader and for marriages. The use of newspapers under beds, inside walls, or in shoes and the sprinkling of salt are related to a rich African heritage. Hag stories are a fragment of a larger story of African heritage. The Hag remedies can prevent a Hag from "tief" (stealing) your soul before "Day Clean" (morning) or drive you "crack-crack (crazy)" and broaden your appreciation of African Culture.

Domesticate the Negro (The Penn School Experiment)

St. Helena Island's Penn School, like many schools on plantations, were started for the education of children and adults in service professions. They usually had African American teachers. The Gullah community started Penn School on Oaks Plantation. Penn was supposed to be relocated on Port Royal Island, but was moved to Brick Church. Brick's one room school eventually became too small for the large student population. Northern churches began sending supplies and missionaries to the school. Eventually, it was relocated on the current Penn Center Campus. The educational focus of Penn started changing during the Civil War and focused upon teaching servitude labor. The Gullah community had the primary ingredients for independent Black businesses and needed to be pushed more in that direction; Instead the Black community was taught to be a dependent labor force educated to serve White peoples.

The Gullah community was not consulted about developing a Black curriculum or how Penn School could serve their educational, social, financial, or political needs. Historically, the school did not offer courses on how the Black community could establish cooperatives, factories, industries, colleges, banks, credit unions or political groups. This may have served the Gullah communities needs more humanely. Instead, the total full force of the government, missionaries, businessmen, created a low-income class of domesticated Negroes in the name of an educational experiment. The boys' "industrial" training meant laborers in crafts and trades that they said would enable the boys (men) to have a dignified living. The girls' (women) domestic science training meant work cleaning White people's houses. Sometimes, the girls were sent to white male private schools, colleges, and dormitories to work and be sexually abused. These jobs for boys and girls were called "working out." This is a term for domestic work, working in fields, hotels, restaurants, picking agriculture foods, working in packing houses, **fish**, crab, oyster and shrimp factories. The domestication of Negroes or school training to "work out" provided jobs for Black to make a living. Servitude jobs were believed to be a way to ensure that the Gullahs would not move to urban areas for jobs. A former instructor at Hampton Institute, Rossa Cooley, was brought to Penn to help make the educational experiment progress.

The Penn School domestication of Negroes was mislabeled a "test" of the Negro's ability to learn skills. Gullahs already had the same skills and used these same skills for 450 years while they were slaves. It is well known that slaves operated, managed, deep sea divers, musicians, supervised, negotiated business deals, translators, were bookkeepers, navigators, teachers, midwives, sailors, carpenters, Blacksmiths, soldiers, craftsmen, agriculturists, and were sold as slaves because of technological skills. These skills, used by free Blacks could inadvertently cause Blacks to be independent. These skills had to be converted to servitude domestic laborers such as shoe repair, brick makers, cobbling, carpentry, butlers, cooks, maids, harness-making, masons, potters, seamstresses, basket-weavers, seamstress, tailors, wheelwrights, blacksmiths, and other skills needed by the white community. Donations, fund-raisers, Philanthropists, and religious groups, including fraudulent and deceptive money activities financed this domestication of the Negro.

Penn School had white groups, businesses, political organizations, and individuals continuously soliciting money to maintain and expand the school and services to the Black community. Penn accumulated large amounts of money from White peoples fundraising and donation schemes, which made a few whites people rich while exploiting the Black students and community. Much of Penn's historical White criminal economic activities are disgusted as benevolent or are falsely documented or not documented. However, the Penn Center Library still houses an abundance of proof of White people's fraudulent scam economic activities. Penn served as a type of off-shore bank, re-cycling money back to White individual and corporation and a means to hide stolen money that used non-profit fundraisers as a disguise. For example, in 1932, the wealth of Penn school was $300,000. This money was supposed to go to the education of the enrolled 36 students and help the community. In the early 1940's, Penn school had 1 million dollars in money and assets, including land in Africa, railroads, textile mills, a utility company and owned rental properties in New Jersey, New York, and elsewhere. These monies amounted to more than enough to educate the small student population, establish Black-owned factories, industries, banks, colleges, etc. However, it is economically clear that the Negroes received none of the benefits from the White thieves in charge of the school. White people used Penn School Negroes as a logo (identifying trademark) similar to the Negroes, Aunt Jemima on the pancake box and Uncle Ben on the rice box. Neither of these Negroes received a penny for their pictures, stimulating millions of dollars in sales. Penn Negroes were similarly used as logo bait to seduce White corporations, White people, and poor Blacks to donate monies.

The Penn School Negro logos (students) were used in a Wilhelmina Lynch (female version of Willie Lynch) strategy. With one exception from the Willie Lynch tactic, it pitted whites against whites. Willie Lynch contains strategies for "seasonin" Africans. "Seasonin" is the cultural castration of Africans in order to give them the state of mind called a "slave" and the chained (chattel) or unchained behavior servitude (must have a White job, education, clothes, food, religion, culture, etc.) to White Supremacy. Incidentally, the Willie Lynch letter was written by Kwabena Ashanti PH. D, retired black psychologist. White Domination support by the belief of White Supremacy, which is protected by White Racism allows Whites as a group to have a superior position over Black People. This superior position was pass down from generation to generation. The wealth created by slavery and the control of Black people's human resources and natural resources was also passed down. Black people are in oppressive captivity (i.e., Sea Island, Diaspora and in Africa) and must follow the laws, rituals and customs of White civilization. Oppressed Black people (chained or unchained) are a "slave". And white privilege allows every White person to directly or indirectly be a Slave Master (controls Black people educational curriculums, rewards and punishment). This is seen in Penn school's continuous series of fundraising frauds and swindles used a cyclical logic diversion, which kept attention away from the White perpetrators of the stealing. The logic cycle started with:

1. Penn School being viewed by the public as a Church operation
2. Then, the Church was viewed as a Black community-based attempt to uplift the former slaves, and then
3. The community was viewed as Penn School thus returning back
   to Step 1 in the cycle.

The cyclic logic diverts attention away from the Whites thieves and makes it impossible to directly blame them for crimes. It would be the same as blaming the Church and the Negroes. It must be kept in mind that the students, teachers, and Gullah residents were not a part of or aware of the scam (fraudulent deceptive operations). In the "Wilhelmina Lynch" scam fund-raisers, political groups, donation accounts, and businesses competed against and with each other to raise money to steal from the Negroes. The White owners of Penn School would get their share of the profits from scams and then give what amounts to peanuts to the Negroes.

In the past, Penn established a White-owned cooperative that serviced the Black community. The community could borrow money, pay interest on their loans and only qualified for loans if they used their land as the collateral. The cooperative sold seeds to Blacks that were donated to the Black community. The donated seeds, damaged fertilizers, tools, and other items were supposed to be given to the Gullahs. The damaged fertilizer destroyed crops, which caused further economic hardship on the Negroes and caused Blacks to default on loans and eventually lose land (collateral), to Whites. Land was also lost due to nonpayment of taxes. For example, Charles E. Jenkins of St. Helena's Island would attempt to pay his $200 land tax, but was told at the tax office that he only had to pay $50. When Charles A. Jenkins would come to pay his $50 taxes, he would be told it was already paid. This eventually would cause both Jenkins to lose their land. Penn's solution to this scam was another scam. Penn raised money to pay the land taxes of the Jenkins' and other Blacks. Of course, Penn would loan the donated money to Blacks at interest and the loan was secured by using the land as collateral. If the Blacks did not have money to pay off the loan, then they would become an indenture slave laborer, share cropper and work to pay off the debt. In some cases, if money from their low wages failed to cover the loan, Penn (i.e., affiliated business or company) would get the land and profit from the free labor. In another scam, Penn convinced the State to build a series of small schools. The Penn affiliated construction company was contracted to build them. The supplies were donated. Penn told the State that each school would cost $200 in construction supplies (was donated = free supplies) and Black labor (which was free). However, upon completion of the schools, Penn overcharged and inflated the price to $800 per school in order to extort more money in the scam. The success of this "Wilhelmina Lynch" money laundry tactic and domestication of the Negroes was well known. White officials from other states, countries, and school systems visited Penn to copy the domestication techniques and the money scams.

Penn Normal Industrial Agriculture School shifted from a normal academic White curriculum of education to crafts and trades between 1900 and 1904. In 1950, Penn School officially ended its educational function. Today, Gullah culture and Penn School is being used to bring tourist dollars to the area. The African Americans that visit the area get a sense of cultural pride. However, the major tourist dollars do directly benefit White Caucasian people's businesses and not the Gullah residents. Gullah culture is becoming a White American tourist business.

No retribution to the Gullah communities has ever been made for past scams and violent crimes perpetrated by Penn's White people.

Gullah Basket Making

Sea grass basket making is an ancient African art form that Gullah slaves brought to America. Basket making was part of the necessary crafts on plantations from Florida's St. John River to North Carolina's Cape Fear. However, more than 90 percent of the basket makers for rice plantations were concentrated in South Carolina and Georgia. A slave with the ability to make coiled grass, plaited palmetto, and split oak baskets sold at higher prices than field laborers. Making grass implements and baskets was a functional part of life that survived slavery because of its artistic value and usefulness. The various African styles and techniques of sea grass baskets symbolized Maat, spirituality and consciousness. Baskets reveal a rich culture, lifestyle, and heritage.

Ancient African baskets date back to 5000 BCE. The African written language Medu Netcher (so-called Hieroglyphics) uses a sea grass basket for the symbol for the letter "K" as well as the letters "nb" and the words "every," "any," and "all." This indicates that basket weaving is at least as old as African languages (5 million years old). In Africa, baskets were used for sieves, storage of food, herbs, utensils, making, art, toys, decorative jewelry, hats and clothing. The ancient African Trans-Atlantic and Trans-Pacific shipping industry, camel and elephant caravans used baskets. The ancient Herb Shops (erroneously called Flower Shops) used sea grass frames for medicinal bouquets, reefs, decorative neck collars clothing, and candle decorations.

The scent from herb stems, roots, and flowers was called aromatic therapy. Aromatic therapy used fragrance from plants mixed with basket weaving grasses. The fragrance from plants were applied to baskets, rugs, and mats. Herbs, such as eucalyptus, sandalwood, chamomile, water lily, clover, licorice, sassafras, fennel, cinnamon, peppermint, rosemary, carob, and lavender were made into the weaving of baskets.

Doctor Athotis, the son of Menes, the Pharaoh of Egypt (3200 B.C.E.) used herbs and woven baskets, jewelry, and utensils. Doctor Imhotep of the Third Dynasty (2980 B.C.E.), Doctor Hesy Ra (2600 B.C.E.) and the female Doctor Preshet (2600 B.C.E.) used sea grass woven items. Incidentally, Doctor Preset was one of the first women doctors in recorded history. Ancient African baskets have been found in the Theban Tomb of the 18th Dynasty, King Tutankhamen (King Tut) 14 B.C.E., King Thuthmosis III, and King Akenaten (Amenophis IV). In the "Feast of the Valley" festival, honoring Queen Hatshepsut, grass woven mats and baskets were used. Ramesse III of Egypt offered bread in a grass bread basket to honor Amun-Ra. His name was said after prayers and was distorted to the word Amen. The usage for grass for baskets, collars, and mats are in the Egyptian Book of the Dead. Paintings in the pyramid and coffin text show the mythological God Osirus and Goddess Isis sitting on thrones in chairs that may be resting on grass mats. In ancient Africa, some baskets were made of Cyperus, Fennel, Lentil, Papyrus, and Dom Palm. In contemporary times, Gullah basket making dates back as far as 1672. Fanners are listed in the Charleston County S.C, register of Wills and Inventories of Noah Serre on May 18, 1730.

Basket making was a family-centered trade. Each family had unique styles of designing grass baskets. Unique designs can be traced to a specific tribe (i.e., Ashanti, Senegambia, Mende, Angolans, Yoruba, Twi, Gullah, etc.). Each individual tribal member added their personal artistic signature to their work. The learning of basket making was experiential (learning by doing). It focused on the basic steps of making a knot, starting a coil, feeding grass, adding new strips of palmetto leaves and finally making the basket "end off." Women usually made household type baskets for serving, storing utensils and food, and decorative chair, tables, art, curtain, floor mats, and functional artifacts. Men usually made large heavy baskets for thatching; reedwork; sieves; fish traps; drying trays; granary utensils; rugs; harvesting of corn, yams, potatoes, rice, and cotton; and bushel baskets. However, during slavery, the demand for the heavier baskets used in field work caused basket making to become mostly a man's art.

The basic grass for basket making is called Rush (Juncus Roemerianus) or needle grass, bulrush, or rushel. It is stronger and more durable than sweet grass or pine straw and grows in sea water marsh. It is harvested by cutting with a rice hook and then dried. It is usually coiled in a bundle and bound together by stitching a binder around the bundle. Usually, the coil starts at the center of the bottom of a basket and the bundles are wrapped over each other like a coiling snake. This spiral coiling snake design symbolizes man's consciousness. It also represents the continuous presence of God in all aspects of life. The wrapping of bound coiled bundles with palmetto leaves is similar to a vine plant wrapping itself around a tree. The other basket making technique of plaiting or the intertwining of grass in a hair braid method symbolized the ancient African Caduceus. The ancient African Caduceus (intertwined snakes) is used as the medical symbol. Single and double-row basket handles resemble the intertwined snakes. The overall repetitive horizontal and vertical designs and units represent birth and rebirth.

The stitching of grass baskets requires that split palmetto or oak is tied onto the previous stitch. The stitch is then pulled through almost to the end of its length. Then, the end of the previous binder are added to the new binder and are tucked between the rows. Next, the new bundle is tightly wrapped with splits before a new stitch is started.

A "nail bone" or "bone" is the tool used to pull the binder through the coil foundation and for making the palmetto strips. Nail bones can be made with bagging needles, rib bones of hogs or cows, broken scissors or the neck of a teaspoon.

The fanner baskets are the most popular. They were usually carried on the head with foodstuff or other items inside. The fanners were used for separating the chaff of the rice from the rice grain before putting it in a mortar with a pestle. Rice pounded in a mortar with a pestle and threshed brown rice was poured into the fanner then tossed up into the air 12 inches or more and then caught in the Fanner or poured into a basket on the ground. This allowed the chaff to be blown away from the brown rice. Fanners can be up to 20 inches in width, 3 inches in height, and have a saucer shape. They are coiled rush, sewn with oak splits or strips of cabbage palm leaves or palmetto butt or leaves. Sometimes, they are made of coiled rice straw and corn shuck. Today, fanners are made for decoration. Gullahs no longer eat the brown rice. Instead, they eat synthetic processed white rice which is robbed of 90 percent of its nutrients and fiber. Once the brown rice is processed into white rice, it becomes a type of synthetic white dirt (junk food similar to bleached white flour, white grits, and white sugar). This is a constipating and diabetes causing food.

Baskets sometimes had grass lids. In ancient African culture, the baskets with the grass "steeple-top" (lid) represent the pyramid or consciousness of God. Typically, most churches have pyramid-shaped steeple roofs. Pyramids produce static electricity aside from symbolizing spirituality. Many baskets have lids such as lunch, trash, bread, sewing, cake, vegetable steamer, and hamper baskets. Aside from these grass-woven baskets, there are handbags, shopping bags, hat boxes, potpourri, and flower baskets.

The African origin of sea grass baskets is noted in the Charleston Chamber of Commerce pamphlet, published in 1938. Alfred Graham, a basket making teacher at Penn School, said that he learned the art from his African father. Basket making is rooted in African civilization. It is an indicator that ancient Africans were not primitive, pagan savages from a dark continent.

Finding of wells, sweet grass basket weaving, and carrying items on the head are parts of African Gullah Culture (Margaret McDonald Sanders)

Gullah Herb Medicine

Gullah herbal medicine is based upon the ancient African bipolar concept of Art (Female Principle) and Science (Male Principle) of holistic medicine. Herb treatments require knowledge of the spiritual, emotional, mental, and physical (holistic) aspects of disease and wellness. Africa is the origin of holistic herb medicine. The oldest books on health are the African books racistly mislabeled and given White European names of the thieves that stole them such as the Kahum Medical Papyrus (1700 BCE), Edwin C. Smith Papyrus (1600 BCE), and Eber Medical Papyrus (1550 BCE). Gullah medicine, due to slavery/ colonialism is diluted because African peoples' languages, holistic medicine, spirituality, and Maat culture was and is constantly made diluted and dysfunctional by White historians and textbook writers. This brief listing of herb remedies can be prepared singularly or in combinations by using the measurement of 1 teaspoon of herb to a cup of water. Herb roots, barks, berries, and seeds are boiled at low heat (simmered) for an hour or more while herb leaves and flowers are put in boiling hot water and allowed to soak (steep) for an hour then strained and drank. These herbs are effective and can be purchased in whole plant, powders, pill or liquid extract form and used singularly or in combination. The asterisk (*) indicates popular herbs used for a remedy.

Arthritis/Rheumatism
Angelica
Cherry Bark
Button Snakeroot
Poke Root (Berries)
Sassafras*
Burdock*
White Willow

Burns/Ulcers(Sores)
Garlic
Cow Dung(Applied)
Comfrey*
Elderberry
Life Everlasting
Sutras

Bites
Elderberry (Apply for Chigger)
Ironweed (Snake)
Angelica Tree (Snake)

Colds/Asthma
Black Root
Boneset
Button Snakeroot
Horehound*
Life Everlasting*
Mullein*
Nightshade
Brown Muckle (Bayberry)
Poke Root
Pine Tar
Speedwell
Sweet Bum (Fruit)
St. John
White Snakeroot
Groundsel bush/White Muckle/Sea Myrtle
Ginger Root

Circulation (Poor)
Bloodroot
Dandelion Root
Needle

Cramps
Mint (Stomach)

Life Everlasting
Sampson's Snakeroot
Ayshaberry/Black Cohosh (Female)

Cuts
Elderberry
Senna (Apply)
Sutras
Burdock

Constipation
Senna*
Okra

Diuretic
Aloe
Kidney Weed
Jerusalem Artichoke
Button Snakeroot
Ginger Root
Parsley

Diabetics
Peach Leaves
Blue Raspberry leaves/Huckleberry/Bilberry*

Female Problems
(Fibroids, Endometriosis. etc.)
Ayshaberry/Black Cohosh (Estrogen)*
Dandelion Root*
Burdock Root*
Red Clover*
Saw Palmetto Berry*
St. John
Nightshade

Fever
Bitter Apple
Boneset
Ironweed
Life Everlasting*
Muckle
Mullein*
Tadawas
White root
Fever (Oil) Bush (Bath)

Griping
Blackberry
Dog Fennel*
Ginger*

Headaches
Indian Shot (Lady's Slipper)
White Willow*

Heart Trouble
Black Cohosh
Hyssop
Chamomile

Hair Rinse
Mistletoe
Pine Needles*
Nettle (Also drank for hair growth) *

High Blood Pressure
Hyssop*
Black Cohosh
Garlic*
Boneset
Saw Palmetto Berries
Spanish Moss (Put in Shoes)

Itch
Hairy Laurel
Chickweed
Measles
Burdock Root
Chickweed
(Chickweed can be used for controlling the appetite and colds)

Menstruation
(Decrease flow)
Brown Muckle (Bayberry)
Cherry Bark
Horse nettle
Comfrey
Red Oak (Pain, douche for prolapsed uterus)
Cotton Root (Small amount eases labor, large amount causes abortion)

Muscle Pain/Sprains
White Willow*
Fennel (Apply to area)
Swamp Grass
Mullein
Boneset
Pain
Life Everlasting (Foot pain)
Mint (Stomach pain)
White Willow (All areas)
Poultices
Clay and Moss
Fennel or Onion and Clay

Sting
Fennel
Tobacco (Apply)
Galax
Burdock

Swelling
Brown Muckle (Bayberry)
Jimson Weed
Mullein
Chinaberry
Ginger Root

Ticks
Red Muckle
Burdock

Tonic
Sassafras
Mullein
Life Everlasting
Ayshaberry
Dandelion Root

Worms
Cloves
Ayshaberry/Black Cohosh
Button Snakeroot
Jimson
Sampson's Snakeroot
Garlic

Warts
(Skin Disease, Fibroids, Endometriosis, Enlarged
Prostate, Sarcoidosis)
Cedar Wood/Thuja
Burdock Root
(Drink and/or apply to area)

RootWork: Dr. Buzzard

Doctor Buzzard is a title given to a Root Worker. The Sea Islands African American communities, slave plantations, and ancient African civilization had Root Doctors. Root work currently exists in all Black communities. This aspect of Black culture has been distorted and misunderstood because of "Seasonin" (Brainwash). Slaves lost the original Rites of Passage (educational curriculum) used to enter the healing art and science. They functioned with partial knowledge of the Kemetic herbal prescriptions, spiritual, psychological and emotional cultural methods. There have been many to exploit and misrepresent holistic medical science. Here are a few examples of Root work prescriptions.

Luck:

Get a red onion. Cut a small hole in the onion. Put five coins in the hole. Soak the onion, with the coins in it overnight in a tea made of High John the Conqueror (Bloodroot, or Red Root). The next day, take the coins out of the onion. Take the coins with you when you gamble (Fantasy sports, Bingo, Lottery, etc.). The coins make your five fingers lucky.

Escape a Love Spell:

Get a picture of the person or a witness, such as a piece of their hair or something they have touched or worn. Mix the witness with graveyard dirt and ashes from burnt a plant and throw the mixture at a crossroads or road leading out of town.

Turning de Tricks:

Write the person's name on paper three times backwards. Put the paper and Devil's Claw herb in a jar. If the trick or spell involves your car, money, job, always losing things, sex, etc., then write that word three times backwards, and put the paper in the jar. Bury the jar in the cemetery at night.

The psycho-spiritual emotional practitioners of this holistic science have many titles, such as Root Doctor, Conjurer, Santerian (usually Cuban, Puerto Rican), Murdumagas Abinzas (Sudan), Hoodoo, Voodoo (Haiti), Shaman, Condomble (Brazil), JuJu, Curanderos, Priest/Priestess, Shango (Trinidad), Ngangas, Mojo, Doctor Buzzard (Sea Islands), Pukumina and Obea (Jamaica), Sorcerer Marabouts, Occultist, etc. Many honestly treat the body, mind, emotion, and spirit, while some are perpetrating a fraud exploiting the food illiteracy, health ignorance, and emotional weakness of the people. These practitioners use herbs, witnesses, rituals, ceremonies, incantations, psychic ability, trances, theater, music, hypnotism, eggs, nails, parts of bushes or trees, water, metal, graveyard dirt, shells, bones, forks, shoes, hats, stones, coins, drums, candles, incense, bells, psychology, electromagnetic aura science, spells, etc. There are many ancient books (erroneously called Papyrus) that documents this art such as Leyden Papyrus, Ebers Papyrus, Salt Papyrus, Ani Papyrus (Egyptian Book of the Dead), etc.

The practitioner may use the energy pathway of a person which is also called acupuncture meridians, chakras, chi, prana, Akasic, aura, life force, etc. The neurological pathways are specific and similar to an individual's fingerprints and DNA. This nerve imprint (aura, DNA) is left upon anything an individual touch, feels, fears, and believes. It is on the individual's photograph, hair, clothing, audio tape of an individual's voice, their handwriting, etc. It is sometimes called a DNA witness to an individual's existence. Historically, there have been many Africans that have used the science.

In history, many African Root Work Practitioners were part of the counterattacks (so-called slave rebellions and revolts) against the Race War. The War was caused by the stealing and murdering White military invasion colonization of Africa and enslavement of Blacks. The ancient East Indians and Chinese, Greeks, Romans, Asians, and the combined European countries continuous military invasion, murder, enslavement, inferiorization and colonialization of all Black people and their land are, by definition, a Race War. Black warriors that fought in the Race War, such as Toussaint L'Ouverture, were considered Root Doctors. He used conjuring to give his Haitian army added strength to fight for their freedom.

In 1751, conjurer and psychic Chief/Priest MacKandal of Haiti, was a military scientist and root worker practitioner that used his skills to organize a counterattack against French tribes that controlled France's Slave plantation. In 1791, conjurers and military scientists Priest Bookman and Lamour Derance, used spells in their counterattack (Revolt). In 1822, the Minister of Defense for Denmark Vesey, was a practitioner named Gullah Jack. He used his root work and military skills in the counterattack against White enslavers in Charleston, South Carolina. In 1831, Nat Turner's counterattack against the slavery business, in Virginia, involved practitioners. David Walker was known to be a Pan-Africanist and a practitioner of the Art/Science of Psycho-Emotion-Spirituality and Root Work. George Washington Carver, a former slave, plant hybridizer and chemist, used conjuring and positive thinking to emotionally and psychologically to free himself of the brainwashing of slavery. He was known to say that the plants told him what to do. The many herbalists, midwives, and conjurers were able to emotionally influence and alter events and lives of enslaved Blacks because they used Root Work technology that is a fundamental part of African culture.

The root worker practitioner must diagnose the disease, find the cause, and prescribe a remedy. They must distinguish whether the disease is from natural causes, (diet, drugs, an organ malfunction, stress, food addiction, toxins, etc.) and or supernatural (i.e., ancestors, Arisha, spirit illness, a double cross = KA), and or preternatural, (spell, jinx, curse, hex, etc.).

After the practitioner diagnoses the illness, they must
- Tell who do it to you (Who Do = Hoodoo)
- Find the witness (item used for the curse, such as egg, bottle, wood, food, etc.)
- Tell whether it is a Hex, Spell, Evil Eye, Curse, Double Cross, or whether another practitioner was paid to do it.
- Reverse the Hex = Double the Cross, Turn the Bible, Turn the Trick;
- Give a treatment and remedy = cure.

It is a very sensitive emotional, spiritual science, and puts the practitioner in just as much danger as the client (victim).

Many Africans are too ashamed of conjurers and deny that spells exist and are too afraid to challenge the existence of Root Work. There are those that did not believe that the African science of acupuncture or hypnotism actually worked. If they were hypnotized in front of an audience and after being taken out of a hypnotic trance, they would still deny that hypnotism worked. Many Africans have been and/or are currently under a conjurer's spell. They mistranslate and mis-explain conjurers' spells as bad luck, fate, and punishment for past deeds. Many adult and children's physical, emotional, and mental illnesses are caused by spiritual imbalances, emotional injuries, or conjurers. These illnesses are ignorantly treated with surgery, drugs, and psychology.

The majority of the Doctor Buzzard practitioners are sincere and use some form of Maat (reciprocity, justice, righteousness, solidarity, hope, fairness) in helping people. Historically, Africans never have had fear of spirits, magic, spells, curses, hoodoo, mojo, or the metaphysical (supernatural). Africans have accepted that harm could be done by unseen forces, emotions, and/or negative thinking. Most of the African holistic practitioners, midwives, naturopaths, herbalists and nutritionist know of the conjurer science. Some use it and others do not. The African focus has shifted away from healing Post Traumatic Slavery Disorder and shifted to divination, psychics, fortune-telling, evil tricks, love potions, sacrifices, luck, winning money, etc. The stores exploit this Africanism and Post Traumatic Slavery Disorder by charging high prices for conjurer artifacts that are believed to change life's circumstances such as cheap egg-dyed water, candles, alcohol and water mixtures, white sugar mixtures, synthetic chemicals, decorative and medicinal herbs and harmless homemade-type concoctions. The true emotional value and holistic power of this African science is being polluted, commercialized, destroyed and put in a cultural crisis.

The isolation of Gullahs on the Sea Islands has allowed them to keep aspects of the African culture and conjurer science alive. Many traces of Root Work practices are alive among all Black People. Many Black people deny that it exists because they have become Afropeans (Seasonin = Civilized = European Domesticated = Coconuts = White inside and Black outside skin). It is similar to the fragmented trace of the Council of the Elders (Wise).

During slavery, the prisoners of the Race War (slaves) would meet at a large tree or in a slave cabin to discuss and debate community issues, marriage problems, bank money, solve conflicts, counsel others, and argue issues. In the cities, the meetings would be held under a special tree and in absence of a tree, the meetings would be held on the corner. The children would gather on the corner and imitate the meetings of the Elders. Boys who would have mock meetings on the corner, imitating the Elders are called Corner Boys. The original cause of the mock meetings is lost and the conversation has taken on forms of self-hatred, cursing Mother Africa (referred to as "Your Momma") and reinforcement of Slavery Trauma. The "Dozens" is played on the corner. The "Dozens" is a slave game of belittling and degrading each other in a humorous competitive fashion. The participants try to make the audience onlookers laugh. Originally, the mentally and physically diseased or handicapped Africans were sold by the Dozen at slave auctions. The Auctioneer would describe the slave's defect. For example, this slave is so retarded that he cannot chew and walk at the same time. The children, in their mock Elders meeting behavior, are pointing back to slavery and African history, and culture. The traces of the Council of Elders cannot be denied just as Gullah African American culture and conjurers can still be found interwoven into the fabric of African American lifestyles.

Index

W

War, 11, 39, 43, 44, 53, 114, 116
Warts, 111
WATERMELON, 86
weaving, 38, 101

West Africa, 11, 16
whites, 11, 13, 34, 39, 43, 46, 47, 48,
   52, 53, 54, 59, 60, 63, 66, 88, 96,
   97, 98, 99, 100
Willie Lynch, 97
Worms, 111

Bibliography

Adams. J.T. Dictionary of American History. New York: Schribener and Sons, 1940.

Amponsah, K. Topics on West African Traditional Religion. Accra, Ghana: McGraw-Hill, 1974.

Aptheker, H. Afro-American History: The Modern Era. Citadel Press, Inc., 1971.

Avalon Hill Game Company. Baltimore, Maryland.

Baskin, W. Dictionary of Black Culture. Philosophical Library, Inc., 1973.

Beaufort Arsenal Museum. Beaufort, South Carolina.

Bierrer, B.W. South Carolina Indian Lore. Columbia, South Carolina: Bert N. Bierrer, 1972.

Boors tin. D. The Discoverers. New York: Random House, 1983.

Carrots, G. The Encyclopedia of American Facts and Dates. T. Crowell Company, 1972.

Conrad, Earl. "General Tubman, Composer of Spirituals," Etude Magazine, LX (May 1942), 305 f.

Crum, M. Gullah Negro Life in the Carolina Sea Islands. Durham, North Carolina: Duke University Press, 1940.

Dabbs, E. Sea Island Diary. Spartanburg, South Carolina: The Reprint Company, 1983.

Fu-Kiau, K., A.M. Lukondo-Wamba. Kindezi: The Kongo Art of Babysitting. New York, NY: Vantage Press, 1988.

Gahlinger, P., Illegal Drugs

Genovese, Eugene. From Rebellion to Revolution. Vintage Books, 1981.

Hayden, Robert. Eight Black American Inventors. Addison Wesley Publishing Company, 1972.

Holt, Thomas. Black Over White. University of Illinois Press, 1979.

Hull, Richard African Cities and Towns Before the European Conquest.

Jones, P.J. South Carolina: One of the Fifty States. Sandpaper Publishers, Inc., 1985.

Joyner, Charles. Down by the Riverside. University of Illinois Press, 1984.

Kane, J. Famous First Fact. New York: The H.W. Wilson Company, 1964.

Koger, L. Black Slaveowners. Jefferson, North Carolina: McFarland and Company, Inc. 1958.

Mannix, Daniel. Black Cargoes: A History of the Atlantic Slave Trade. Viking Press, 1962.

Mcguffey, W. Custom and Government in Lower Congo. Berkeley, California: University of California Press, 1970.

Mitchell, Faith. Hoodoo Medicine. Reed, Cannon and Johnson Company, 1978.

Morrow, Willie. 400 Years Without a Comb. San Diego, California: Black Publishers, 1973.

Morshead, O.F., The Diary of Samuel Pepys. New York: Harper and Brothers, 1926.

New York Times, August 6, 1865.

Nunez, B. Dictionary of Afro-American Civilization. Greenwood Press, 1980.

Parsons, R.T. Religion in African Society. Leiden E. J. Brill, 1904.

Petit, J.P. South Carolina and the Sea maritime and Ports. Charleston, South Carolina: Activities Committee, 1976.

Postell, W.D. The Health of Slaves on Southern Plantations.

Rose, Julio. Heru-Tage Ra Staured Heru-Scope. Cayce, SC: Starlight Communication, 1997.

Rose, W. Rehearsal for Reconstruction: The Port Royal Experiment. Indiana: Boobs-Merrill, 1964.

Siegel, R Intoxification: Life in Pursuit of Artificial Paradise

The South Carolina Historical Chronicle

Tindall, G.B. South Carolina Negroes, 1877-1900. University of South Carolina Press, 1952.

Waring, J.L. A History of Medicine in South Carolina.

Williams, Chancellor. The Destruction of Black Civilization. Chicago, Illinois: Third World Press, 1976.

Made in the USA
Columbia, SC
04 April 2025

56119269R00070